Bodies, Brains, & Boogers

This book is dedicated to Mrs. Amor, my high school biology teacher. Thank you for inspiring me to follow my passion. I wouldn't have become a super scientist without your support!

Published in 2022 by Welbeck Children's
An Imprint of Welbeck Children's Limited,
part of Welbeck Publishing Group.
Based in London and Sydney.
www.welbeckpublishing.com

Design and layout © Welbeck Children's Limited 2022
Text copyright © 2022 Paul Ian Cross
Published by arrangement with Speckled Pen Limited
Illustration © Welbeck Publishing Limited,
part of Welbeck Publishing Group

Writer: Paul Ian Cross, PhD
Illustrator: Steve Brown
Design Manager: Matt Drew
Editorial Manager: Joff Brown
Production: Melanie Robertson

ISBN: 978 1 78312 896 9

Printed in the UK

10 9 8 7 6 5 4 3 2 1

Bodies, Brains, & Boogers

WELBECK

Paul Ian Cross, PhD

Illustrated by Steve Brown

CONTENTS

CHAPTER 1

AWESOME ANATOMY

OUR BODIES ARE WEIRD.

Our **BRAINS** are even **WEIRDER.**

AND our **BOOGERS?** Well, they're just **GROSS.**

Even though bodies are weird and gross, they're also unique. There's no one else like you in the entire world. As a matter of fact, there's no one like you in the **ENTIRE UNIVERSE.**

WHAT MAKES A HUMAN?

ANATOMY is the branch of biology that looks at the structure of organisms and their different parts. The word comes from the Ancient Greek words "ana" which meant "**UP**" and "tomia" which meant "**CUTTING.**"

Put these words together and you have...

DRUM ROLL ... UP CUTTING.

Wait a minute.

Let's try again.

Swap those words around (ahem), and you have...

DRUM ROLL ... CUTTING UP.

Yes, people of the past learned everything we know about the human body from dissecting people!

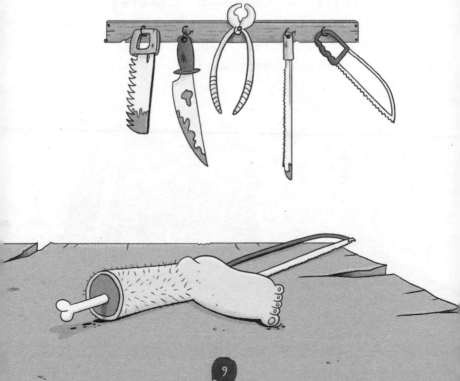

Our bodies are a marvel of nature. But did you know that one of the strangest evolutionary tricks early humans developed was the urge to find things SUPER GROSS?

According to grossologists (they're scientists who study gross stuff—OK, I made up that bit) things that make us go BLECH! were crucial to early human survival. These feelings of disgust protected us from touching or eating the wrong things. It helped early humans to stay away from danger.

Think stinky piles of poop. By being grossed out, we stopped putting our hands in poop, which—as it turns out—is much better for our health. There are lots of gross things lurking in our poop, like bacteria.

UUGH!

So, **GROSSNESS** is **GREAT** *and* **GOOD** **FOR US!**

In this book, you'll learn...

facts about FARTS

trivia about TOENAILS

...and much more!

You have been warned. Get ready. Set. **GROSS!** And prepare to check your **GROSSOMETER** along the way.

GROSSOMETER

I CAN DEAL WITH THIS

NOT COOL DUDE!

GET AWAY FROM ME!

I'M GOING TO PUKE!

HOW GROSS IS THAT?

WHAT IS ANATOMY?

It is the study of the internal structure of living beings—
the bricks and mortar that make human beings US!
But can you already answer these questions about
your greatest living organs?

The Body Parts Puzzle

Q1. Which is the strongest muscle in the human body?

Q2. What is the body's largest organ?

Q3. What makes your heart make a noise?

Q4. Can you identify your largest internal organ?

Q5. What bone structure shows us that humans once
had tails?

Q6. Which part of your body is as hard as a rock?

TURN THE PAGE
UPSIDE DOWN TO SEE
THE ANSWERS!

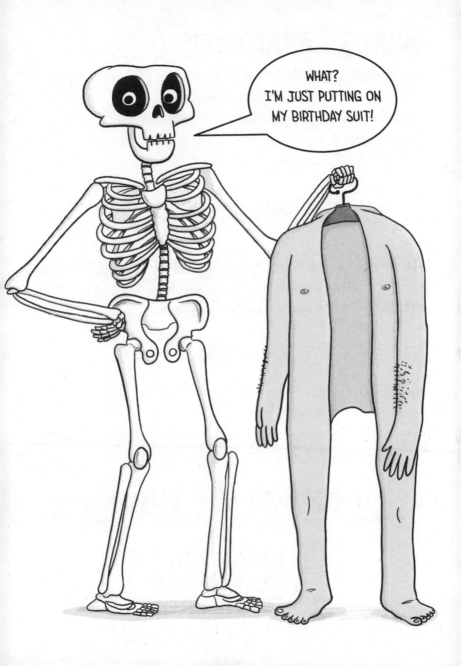

The human body is amazing—a machine that's been perfected through trial and error.

Take a look at your hand.

Go on! Hold it out in front of you.

Now, wiggle the fingers! When you do that, you're looking at the outcome of millions of years of evolution!

Whether you're texting, gaming, or doodling, your hand is what equips you for modern life. The evolution of our **THUMBS**—yes, those stumps with only two bones—are the reason why modern humans evolved to write music, build cities, fly planes, and even travel to the moon.

YOUR THUMBS →
LITERALLY CHANGED
THE WORLD.

Well, not *your* thumbs—although they're probably lovely—but thumbs in general. They made the difference between the beginning of human civilization and humans disappearing off the face of the Earth (probably by being eaten by saber-toothed tigers). OK, maybe that's a little dramatic, but you get the drift.

As it turned out, shorter thumbs and longer fingers were helpful for climbing. But when our ancestors moved from living in the trees to life on the African savanna, they began using their hands in different ways. This changed the actual structure of their hands, and eventually they became much better at **GRASPING**.

Many primates have precise and powerful grips. But early humans took it one step further, using their hands to make tools, and strengthening their thumbs in the process.

GRASP AND GRIP!

Here's a list of things you can do,
thanks to your fantastic thumbs!

- 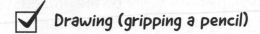 Drawing (gripping a pencil)

-  Painting (holding a paintbrush)

- 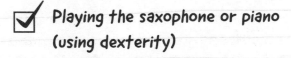 Playing the saxophone or piano
  (using dexterity)

- 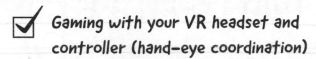 Gaming with your VR headset and
  controller (hand-eye coordination)

MEET LUCY, AN EARLY HOMINID

A hominid is a member of the family *Hominidae*. They include the great apes, like orangutans, gorillas, chimpanzees... and humans too! By studying past humans, we can see how our bodies evolved a certain way, helping to explain why some early humans did better than others.

One of our most famous early ancestors is Lucy, a hominid belonging to a family called *Australopithecus*. It's pronounced:

OSS-TRAY-LO-PITH-E-CUSS!

Not easy—so let's stick with Lucy for now!

Lucy's remains were discovered by Dr. Donald Johanson, an anthropologist, in 1974 at Hadar, a site in the Awash Valley in Ethiopia. Donald named Lucy after his favorite Beatles' song—*Lucy In The Sky With Diamonds*—which was really popular at the time!

Lucy was fully grown when she died, but she was still only 43.3 inches in height. That's about as tall as a four-year-old human girl. She was bipedal, which means she could walk on two legs, but she probably spent a lot of time climbing trees.

Fascinating Facts!

* In biology, we describe different species and families of animals using their Latin names. Latin names are usually written using *italics*.

* Orangutan comes from the Malay words "orang," meaning "person," and "hutan," meaning "forest." They're literally "people of the forest"!

The reason why Lucy and others like her are so important to science is because they may have been some of the first hominids to make very simple tools, around 3.2 million years ago!

The use of these tools resulted in major changes in our anatomy that would eventually lead to **HUMAN CIVILIZATION!**

MODERN HUMANS

Over many millions of years, early humans began using more complex tools. This required better hand-eye coordination. Think about gripping a baseball bat and swinging it at a moving ball—we need to coordinate our hands and eyes to do this.

This meant early humans were also able to learn and develop problem-solving skills. This required bigger and better brains, resulting in the development of COGNITION—the way we acquire knowledge through thought, experience, and the senses.

Cognition was an important first step in helping early humans to develop language! We can only imagine what their first words would have been...

ME. SMASH. WILDEBEEST. ME. GET. YUM YUMS!

The theory of evolution

Evolution is the way that organisms adapt to their surroundings, over many generations, by developing improved characteristics to help them survive.

There were many types of early humans, and some species did better than others. Modern Humans lived alongside other types of humans, such as Neanderthals and Denisovans, but eventually

As humans developed, our species had a competitive advantage over other early human species. Maybe we were better at hunting, or perhaps the areas where we lived had more food available. Whatever it was, these advantages allowed Homo sapiens sapiens—modern humans—to TAKE OVER THE WORLD. Cue EVIL LAUGHTER...

BAHAHAHAHAHA!

Thanks to our thumbs, early humans managed to grow bigger brains, meaning we were better at doing things. That helped us win the great evolutionary race against other species, changing the course of history. Forever.

Now if that doesn't deserve a THUMBS UP, what does?

the Modern Humans were better at adapting to the environment and out competed these other groups. Imagine a race where Modern Humans won the gold medal, Neanderthals won silver, and the Denisovans won bronze, while the other early humans didn't win anything. Unfortunately, in this race of evolution, anything less than a gold medal meant CERTAIN DEATH.

WHAT MAKES A HUMAN?

Build a human, using the building blocks of life!

AMAZING ATOMS: Humans, like most things, are made up of atoms. Different types of atoms are called elements. These elements include:

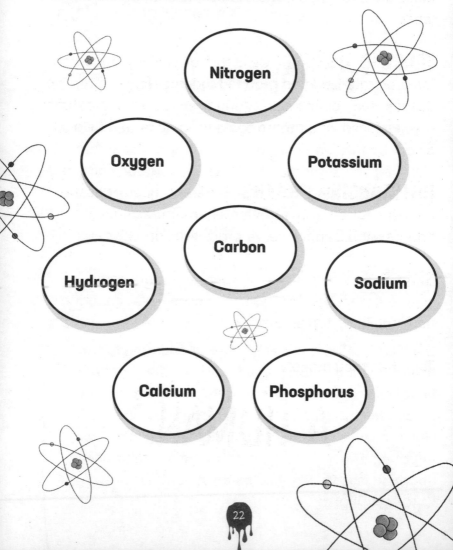

Nitrogen

Oxygen

Potassium

Carbon

Hydrogen

Sodium

Calcium

Phosphorus

COOL CELLS: The body's building blocks are called cells. Each human has over 37 trillion of them! That's a lot, by the way. That's 4,805 times more than the number of people who live on Earth! Imagine that! There are many types of cells, all with their own unique jobs to do, from detecting light (eye cells) to creating new life (sperm and egg cells).

TERRIFIC TISSUES: Cells that all perform the same job are organized and grouped together forming terrific tissues, such as the skin. Many tissues are solids, some are semisolid, and others come in liquid form—like our blood!

OUTSTANDING ORGANS: Different types of tissue combine together to form larger structures called organs such as your heart, brain, liver, and kidneys.

SUPER SYSTEMS: There are twelve main body systems, each with its own unique job to do, ensuring you stay in tip top shape!

Together, they make...

A HUMAN.

SUPER CELLS

The human body contains over 200 types of cells, such as nerve cells, blood cells, hair cells, bone cells, fat cells, and even eye cells...

Eye cells can be divided into two types: rods and cones. Rod cells help us to see in poor light, whereas cones let us see in color. These "photoreceptors" detect light, and convert it into electrical signals that travel through our neurons to reach the optic nerve. Our eyes are the most advanced camera known to humans—even better than your brand-new smartphone!

Fat cells are important for energy storage and are mainly found under the skin and around the organs. We now understand that too many fat cells around our organs is bad for us, so that's why cardiovascular exercise is important—it keeps those fat cell numbers in check!

Blood cells are used to carry oxygen around the body and collect carbon dioxide. They have a limited lifespan and are replaced every 120 days.

Neurons are nerve cells that transmit signals to and from all parts of the body. They make up the nervous system that links up with the body's supercomputer: our brilliant brain!

Bone cells are made inside the bone marrow, deep inside the structure of our bones. As these cells develop and grow, they harden, making the bone nice and strong. Bone marrow is a semisolid tissue and is spongy in nature. In birds and mammals, bone marrow is where most new blood cells are produced!

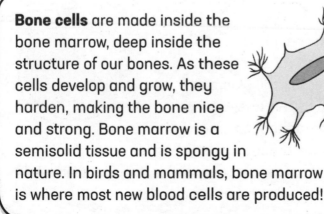

OUR AMAZING BODIES

Here are our twelve main body systems, each with its own unique job to do!

Skin, Hair, & Nails

Muscular

Skeletal

Digestive

Urinary

Endocrine

26

Nervous

Cardiovascualar

Respiratory

Lymphatic

Immune

Reproductive

27

THE CIRCLE OF LIFE...

Every organism on Earth has a lifecycle, from the biting mosquitos that only live for a week, to the lion who lives for thirty years or so, to your great Aunt Mabel, who's **101** and still going strong!

Biologists generally agree that for something to be defined as living it must have some key anatomical elements:

1. Movement: from bacteria to trees, all organisms move in a variety of ways.

2. Respiration: getting and expending energy.

3. Sensitivity: responding to conditions such as heat and light.

4. Growth: Growing, developing, and changing.

5. Reproduction: reproducing and passing on useful characteristics to offspring.

6. Excretion: getting rid of waste, like pee and poop!

7. Nutrition: taking in or making food and absorbing important nutrients.

You can remember all seven criteria from the LIFE LIST using the acronym... MRS. GREN!

...AND DEATH

ALL GOOD THINGS MUST COME TO AN END.

Every organism's lifecycle ends with death. It's a difficult fact of life. It's especially difficult when we lose someone close to us, but that's why we must enjoy every moment, appreciating our loved ones.

And think of it this way—when we learn about our **WONDERFUL WORLD**, and know that each of us are part of the incredible story that is **PLANET EARTH**, it makes us realize how special and lucky we are to be experiencing life. Life as we know it, anyway.

Life is precious. We're all unique. It has taken millions of years for us to be this way. The fact that we're here—breathing, burping, and farting—on this flying ball of rock, traveling around a massive ball of burning gas, is **INCREDIBLE**. We need to make every single day count!

Mrs. Gren

WE ALL GOTTA GO SOMETIME!

Did you know...

✳ Your skin has over 1,000 species of bacteria living on it.

✳ Teeth are considered part of your skeletal system, but are not considered bones.

✳ Your heart beats around 100,000 times a day.

✳ Your body has over 600 muscles.

✳ Your longest—and strongest—bone is the femur in your leg.

✳ Your fingernails grow faster than your toenails.

✳ You produce enough spit to fill two bathtubs every year!

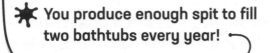

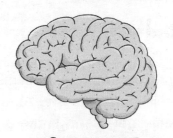

CHAPTER 2

BRILLIANT BRAIN

Your **BRAIN** is the most **ADVANCED SUPERCOMPUTER** known to **HUMANKIND.**

It's made up of vast networks and connections so complicated it's impossible to imagine. This supercomputer has the ability to process billions of things every second, all at the same time! But it's not made of plastic, metals, or microchips.

It's a massive watery **BLOB**—it's squishy and squashy and slimy and wrinkly and **GROSS** and is actually 70 percent water! The remaining 30 percent is made of proteins, fats, sugar, and salt.

BREAKING DOWN THE BRAIN

Thanks to your brilliant brain, you can think about things, see the world around you, remember stuff, and experience feelings. That's why zombies are so obsessed with them—they clearly have great taste!

THE BRAIN'S TO-DO LIST

The brain has many different parts. Each part is responsible for its own unique job. A typical to-do list for the brain might be...

- ☑ remember to do your homework (memory)

- ☑ experience joy on a summer's day (feelings)

- ☑ create a story about zombies eating brains in your mind (imagination)

- ☑ write your zombie-brain-eating story down (movement and dexterity)

- ☑ run away when a real zombie breaks into your house and reaches for your... BRAIN. (the "face or flight response")

BRAIN ANATOMY

Let's take a look at the different parts of the brain and learn about what each part does.

BIG BLOB:
CEREBRUM (this is made up of smaller blobs called lobes). They are the...

- Frontal Lobe (controls thinking, speaking, moving)
- Parietal Lobe (controls touch, and pain..OUCH!)
- Temporal Lobe (controls hearing and recognition)
- Occipital Lobe (helps with seeing)

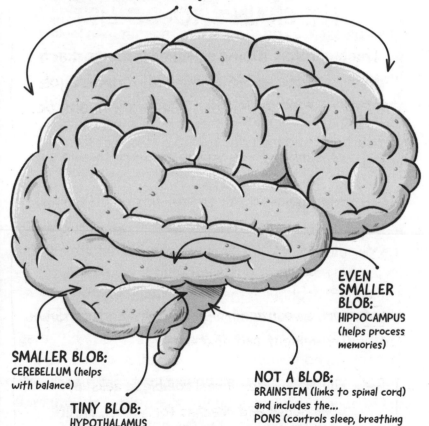

EVEN SMALLER BLOB:
HIPPOCAMPUS (helps process memories)

SMALLER BLOB:
CEREBELLUM (helps with balance)

TINY BLOB:
HYPOTHALAMUS (makes us realize we're hungry or thirsty)

NOT A BLOB:
BRAINSTEM (links to spinal cord) and includes the...
PONS (controls sleep, breathing and swallowing)

Greek lesson!

The word "*neuro*" is Greek for "nerve" so brain scientists are called neuroscientists and brain surgeons are called neurosurgeons! Neuroscientists have mapped hundreds of new areas of the human brain, and they learn and understand more every year!

Scientists use a variety of fancy machines to look at someone's brain. This is super important to check for signs of disease, like a brain tumor. A CT scan (sometimes called a CAT scan) doesn't involve several cats licking your head. It stands for Computed Tomography and includes taking a series of X-ray images of your brain.

MAGNETIC MRI

MRI stands for Magnetic Resonance Imaging. Instead of using radiation, an MRI uses a magnetic field to capture an image. Patients aren't allowed to take any metal into an MRI scanner. If they did, it would fly toward the machine because of the powerful magnetic forces involved. People have been seriously injured when they forgot they had coins in their pockets, or even worse, metal implants inside their bodies they forgot to tell the nurse about! The magnetic force can move the implant across the body, causing terrible damage! ARGH!

HOW BRAINS CHANGED

Did you know that the human brain is smaller now than it was 100,000 years ago? Wait a minute, surely if we're more intelligent today then we need the **BIGGEST BRAINS**? Well, not necessarily.

As our brains changed and developed, they became ridged and wrinkled, meaning they had more surface and volume when compared to a flat-surface brain. So the fashionistas are right, after all...sometimes less **IS** more!

LUCY

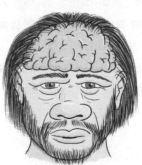

NEANDERTHAL

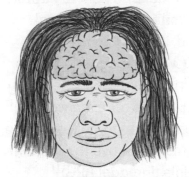

DENISOVAN

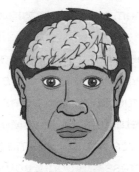

HOMO SAPIENS

BRAIN'S BUILDING BLOCKS

Supercomputers need to have lots of parts. There are about 86 billion brain cells and another 80 billion supporting cells in the brain. That's A LOT of cells! The brain cells are called NEURONS and the supporting cells are called GLIAL cells.

HOP THE GAP!

Neurons do not actually stick together. They have tiny gaps between them called SYNAPSES. Electrical signals move along the neuron, and chemicals called neurotransmitters travel across the tiny gap.

There are several types of neurotransmitters. They affect our mood in different ways. Serotonin is known as the "happy" neurotransmitter, as it makes us feel good!

When these chemicals arrive at the other side, they turn on the next neuron. It's like flicking a light switch! Then, the electrical signal continues on its journey...

VERY QUICKLY

...at around 275 miles per hour. That's as fast as a small aeroplane!

Neurons look like trees...

- branches on one side

- a long trunk in the middle

- lots of roots!

Branches

Trunk

Roots

Close up!

When the cell is activated, electricity moves down the branches, along the trunk and into the roots. It all happens in a FLASH. That's right, your brain is both squishy and...ELECTRIC.

SUPER SIGNALS!

The brain sends signals that zap through your nervous system at lightning-fast speeds. There are three main ways your head does this. It...

1. Receives signals from the five senses (sight, smell, sound, taste, and touch—see Chapter 5!)

2. Passes signals from one part of the brain to another

3. Sends signals out to other parts of the body

SPINE SCIENCE

The Nervous System links your brain to the rest of your body. If your brain tells you to do something, it sends the right signal to the right place. The signal leaves the brain, then travels through the brain stem and into the spinal cord—where it shoots off to one of the many branches of the nervous system.

Fascinating Facts!

☀ There are about **100 TRILLION** neural connections in your brain, which is about 1,000 TIMES more than the number of stars in the Milky Way!

☀ By the time you're an adult you'll have about 45 MILES of nerves in your body.

☀ Nerves in your body can be as thin as a hair or as thick as your thumb.

BMAIL, A BIT LIKE EMAIL

Brain signals are similar to sending emails to your friends. Let's say that you are the brain, and your hand is the friend:

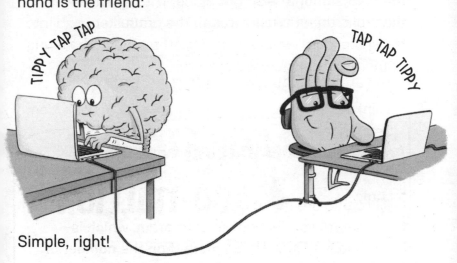

Simple, right!

You send an email that says "wave", and it pings all the way through the nervous system to your hand. Your hand opens the message and reads it right away, gets the message, and waves!

Pain signals travel the opposite way. For example, if you're holding a hot cup and are about to burn yourself, the message is sent from your hand to your brain. Pain signals can travel to your brain four times faster than cars travel on the highway! They need to travel fast so that your brain can tell you to put the cup down quickly. Don't drop it! **SMASH**. Oops. Too late.

SCIENCE OR ART?

Many years ago, some scientists believed that people are more mathematician than they are Mozart, or the other way around—that you're either scientifically minded, or more artistic. But is this actually true?

SCIENTIST'S BRAIN?
Thinking in Words
Sequences
Mathematics
Facts
Logic

ARTIST'S BRAIN?
Feelings and Visualization
Imagination
Intuition
Rhythm
Arts

ALL ABOARD THE STEAM TRAIN!

You know what STEM is: Science, Technology, Engineering and Mathematics. But there's something way better than that. And that's STEAM!

Science
Technology
Engineering
Arts
Mathematics

Did you know?

Only one in a hundred people can write just as well with their left hand as their right? These talented individuals are called ambidextrous.

This is STEM plus the arts, such as music, dance, drama, visual arts, or design. The main difference between STEM and STEAM is STEM focuses on scientific concepts whereas STEAM also includes art and other creativity. Like learning mathematics using dance, or understanding how a virus works by building a model out of papier mache!

STEAM is not new, though. Leonardo Da Vinci was known for combining the sciences with art, helping him make breakthroughs and discoveries. By using STEAM, we can all combine learning with our creativity!

Turns out we **CAN** be both a scientist **AND** an artist. We all have different personalities and talents, and there's no reason to suggest this has anything to do with the "type of brain" we have. As we've seen with STEAM, a combined approach to learning is best and means everyone can thrive in both the sciences and the arts!

THANKS FOR THE MEMORIES!

Remember the best birthday party you ever had? No, not the one with the creepy clown. The one when you went to **LASER QUEST! ZAP ZAP!** Wasn't that the best day? Well, the reason you are able to return to your happy place and relive those wonderful moments (except when you got zapped at the end) is all thanks to your memories. They're pretty awesome, aren't they!

Memories are like a virtual scrapbook: images, experiences, and feelings stored on your brain's hard disk drive. All you need to do is think of the memory and it pops right into your head. Your brilliant brain brings

back all the sights, sounds, feelings, and emotions from that moment in time. Hopefully good, but sometimes, not so good (stop thinking about the creepy clown).

So how do memories work? Firstly, you experience something, like your birthday party, and your neurons start to flash brightly! Your brain labels the memory with "party" or "creepy clown" and files it away. It goes into short-term storage. As time progresses, it is moved into long-term storage. Once filed there, it's ready to pop right back out at a moment's notice. Those neurons labelled "party" or "creepy clown" flash back on, and you relive the experience all over again!

HOW HUGE WAS THE CLOWN'S HARD DRIVE? 100 GIGGLE-BYTES!

BRAIN FREEZE!

Have you ever eaten too much ice cream all at once and you suddenly get that weird tingling feeling in your head? That's **BRAIN FREEZE**, also known as...

SPENOPALATINE GANGLIONEURALGIA!

This strange sensation is your brain recognizing a change in temperature and getting ready to prepare your body.

Maybe your brain actually thinks you're back in the Ice Age with your cave family and your pet mammoth, Milly. Rather than allowing you to freeze to death, your brain increases blood flow rapidly. This makes you slow down. Cave people who did too much in freezing temperatures quickly became tired and probably didn't last very long.

The brain freeze is like putting on the brakes. It's saying **TAKE IT EASY** while we deal with these changes. Luckily for us, eating an ice cream on the beach doesn't last as long as the Ice Age did, and the feeling soon passes!

THE BRILLIANT BRAIN

Did you know that...

- Almost 50 percent of a kid's energy is used to power their brain.

- Reading aloud and reading silently use different parts of the brain.

- Exercise is as good for your brain as it is for your body.

- As people age, those who use their brains less lose brain matter. So USE IT. OR LOSE IT.

- Sleep is important for the processing of memories.

- Parts of the brain light up when someone is shown a picture of a loved one! Aww!

- When you're awake, your brain produces enough power to light a small light bulb! How illuminating!

True or false?

You only use 10 percent of your brain!

FALSE! This is a myth—in fact, you use most of your brain, most of the time. We all do!

TAPEWORM TALES!

Meet *Taenia solium*, a species of tapeworm. Humans can be infected by these critters by eating pork contaminated with its eggs. Sometimes, the larvae (tapeworm babies) make their way to the **BRAIN** where they feed, causing damage and terrible seizures!

CHAPTER 3

SKELETON SALUTE

Your **SKELETON** is the **STRUCTURE** that **SUPPORTS** and **SHAPES** your **BODY**.

The skeleton is made up of **206 BONES**. This fantastic frame is essential for movement. It allows us to skip, dance, fly kites, and do a somersault down a hill.

This framework is also important for the protection of our internal organs. It's a suit of armor that keeps everything inside safe.

Without our skeleton, the body would collapse in a heap. But surprisingly, it's not as rigid as you would imagine. Flexible joints between strong bones allow the body to move in incredible ways.

SKULL AND CROSSBONES

Pirates love skulls, plastering them all over their flags. Look, we get it—skulls are awesome.

They house our brilliant brains, protecting everything that makes us an individual. Think of your skull like a shield, protecting the blob of tissue and water inside.

HOW MANY BONES MAKE A SKULL?

ONE?

NO!

The skull is made up of **TWENTY-TWO** different pieces, all joined together like a jigsaw puzzle.

These pieces don't fuse together until **AFTER** we're born! Can you believe that? If they did, a baby's head wouldn't be able to make it down the mother's birth canal during labor. Babies' heads need to be flexible enough to squeeze through! They are made to be squishy.

But once we grow up, these bones fuse together and become rock solid. The only part of the skull that can still move around is the jaw, which is just as well—as eating a massive breakfast would be impossible otherwise!

Collecting Collagen

Bone has a protein called collagen inside it. Collagen is the most common protein in the body, making up about 30% of all protein! Collagen is essential for healthy bones, muscles, skin, and tendons. Collagen wears out over time and needs to replace itself. It can take years to completely recycle all the collagen in your skeleton!

FABULOUS FOSSILS

We've learned a lot about human evolution from bones. We know how our fantastic thumbs developed by looking at Lucy's hands. And we've learned how we won the evolutionary race by comparing our skulls with Neanderthals and the Denisovans. Bones have also taught us about animals that have been extinct for thousands or millions of years, like woolly mammoths and...dinosaurs!

GIVE A DOG A BONE

Why do dogs like bones so much? Well, it's probably all the juicy bone marrow, made up of collagen!

Bones come in many different shapes and sizes, depending on where they are in the body.

* **LONG BONES** like the thigh bone (femur) support the body's weight

* **SHORT BONES** (tarsals) provide stability in the hands and feet

* **FLAT BONES** like the shoulder blade (scapula) act as a shield protecting vital organs

* **IRREGULAR BONES** have complex shapes and do a variety of jobs. Think about the vertebrae in your spine!

* **SESAMOID BONES** such as the knee bone (patella) protect tendons and joints from wear and tear

From Big To Small

The longest, and strongest, bone in the human body is the thigh bone.

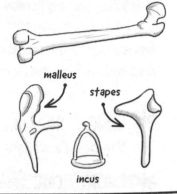

The smallest are the three bones of the inner ear. They're called the malleus, incus, and stapes.

malleus

stapes

incus

The biggest thigh bone ever discovered belongs to a species of sauropod dinosaur called the Argentinosaurus. Argentinosaurus means "lizard from Argentina" named after where it was first discovered. This dinosaur's thigh bone is taller than the average person!

THE SPINE

Dangling down from your skull is your SPINE. This row of 33 bones is a feat of engineering. It protects the spinal cord, a vital link between your brilliant brain and the rest of your body. If the spinal cord is damaged, then the brain can't communicate with the body anymore. This can result in paralysis (the loss of the ability to move some or all of your body). So the spine is SUPER important.

HOW DOES THE SPINE BEND?

The spine is super bendy thanks to 33 little bones called vertebrae. It's pronounced "VER-teb-ray." But that pales in comparisssssssson to the python. They have around six hundred vertebrae and about 1,800 bones!

DO ALL ANIMALS HAVE BACKBONES?

Animals with backbones are called vertebrates. Did you know that not all animals have backbones? Organisms without spines are called invertebrates. Around 97 percent of animals on Earth fall into this group. They include animals like flies and jellyfish, so anything squishy. That means the remaining 3 percent of animals, including humans, are vertebrates. So, we're part of an exclusive club!

Fascinating Facts!

✹ Humans and giraffes have the same number of vertebrae in our necks!

✹ The spinal cord weighs about 1.25 oz—about the same weight as a small egg.

✹ The name coccyx (tailbone) is Latin and comes from "Kokkux"—the Greek word for cuckoo—because the tailbone is shaped like a beak!

HOORAY FOR HANDS!

The hands are full of bones, and that's because we need them to move in certain ways. It all goes back to how our thumbs developed. Over time, our hands became more complex.

Your wrist alone is made up of eight separate bones, and then there's your digits:

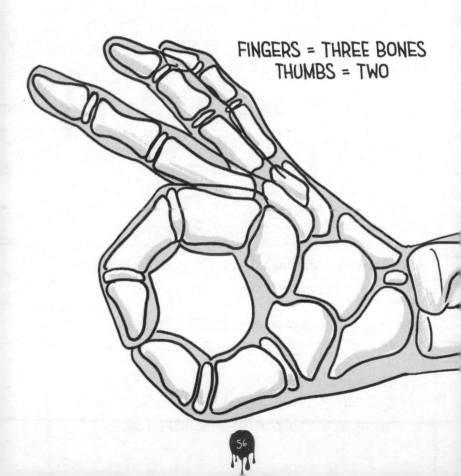

FINGERS = THREE BONES
THUMBS = TWO

Considering what our fantastic thumbs do for us, they don't have much in the bone department. But as we know, less is more. The thumbs are the strongest of the digits thanks to these awesome bones.

FABULOUS FINGERS

Have you ever wondered why your fingers are different lengths? Humans have small palms and short fingers compared to other apes. The different lengths allow us to grip things with **SUPER STRENGTH**. It's even called the **POWER GRIP!**

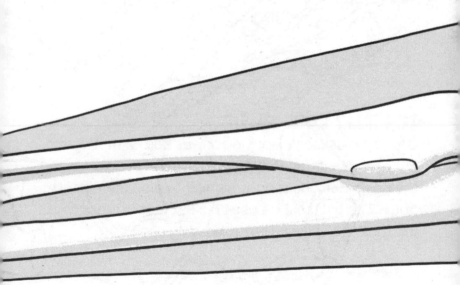

FOOT A SOCK IN IT

Feet are more complex than they look. Remember, they need to support the entire weight of your body.

The flexibility of a foot allows your weight to spread in different ways, whether you're on your tiptoes or sprinting for the bus so you're not late for school.

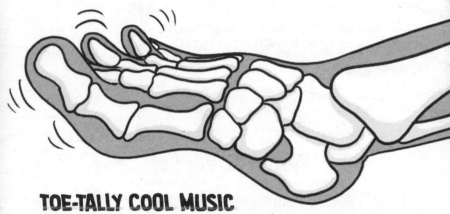

TOE-TALLY COOL MUSIC

German musician Felix Kleiser was born with no arms, but always wanted to play an instrument. So from the age of four, he taught himself to play the French horn...with his toes! He uses his left foot to press the instrument's valves. That's toe-tally cool!

TOE THE LINE

Our toes are important to support us while we walk. But we actually walk using the soles of our feet—unlike cats, who walk using their tippy toes!

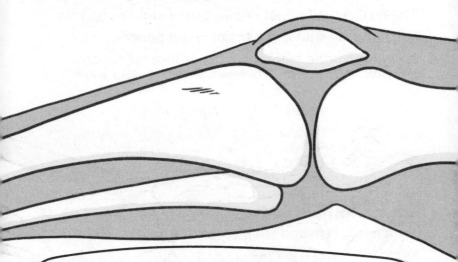

Fun Feet Facts!

✳ The average person walks between 8,000 to 10,000 steps per day. That adds up to about 115,000 miles over a person's life!

✳ There are more than 8,000 nerves in the feet.

✳ Your feet have over 250,000 sweat glands on them, leaking half a pint of sweat every day. That's why they get SUPER STINKY!

JOINING UP

Joints are the places where two bones connect. There are an incredible **360 JOINTS** in the human body. There are many different types, such as:

- **Synovial joints**, like those in your knees

- **Ball and socket joints**, like those in your hips

- **Hinge joints**, like those in your fingers, elbows, and toes

COOL CARTILAGE: this tissue is not quite as hard as bone but is firm and spongy. It's a connective tissue, found in between joints.

LOVELY LIGAMENTS: they are another type of connective tissue that connects bones to other bones.

TERRIFIC TENDONS: they are a very strong, flexible tissue similar to rope! They connect our bones to our... marvelous muscles!

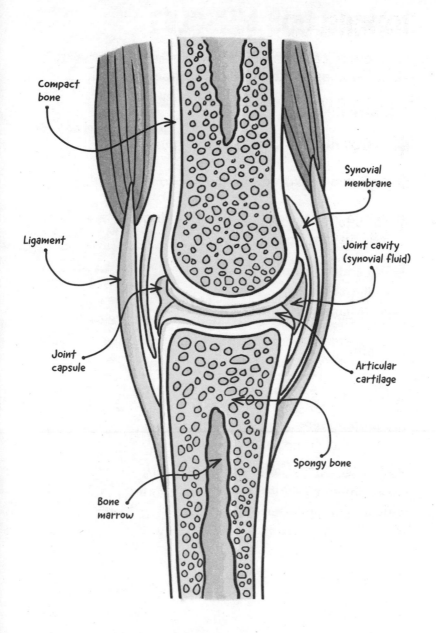

Compact bone

Ligament

Joint capsule

Bone marrow

Synovial membrane

Joint cavity (synovial fluid)

Articular cartilage

Spongy bone

MARVELOUS MUSCLES

Our muscles sit over our skeleton, and underneath our skin. There are three types of muscle:

 Skeletal

Smooth

Cardiac (heart muscle)

Muscles are important for:

1. Movement—from smiling to running to throwing a ball!

2. Breathing

3. Eating

4. Pumping blood around your body!

The smallest muscles in the body are in the inner ear, while the largest is the gluteus maximus, in the buttocks!

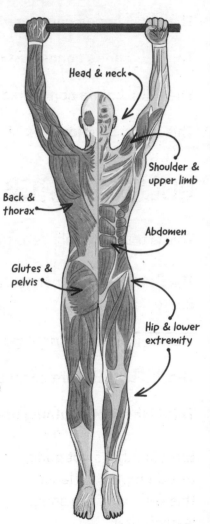

Head & neck

Shoulder & upper limb

Back & thorax

Abdomen

Glutes & pelvis

Hip & lower extremity

THE SKELETON DANCE!

Let's learn science through the medium of dance.
Maestro, play the music!

The FOOT bone's connected to the leg bone.

The LEG bone's connected to the knee bone.

The KNEE bone's connected to the thigh bone.

This is the skeleton dance!

HOLD ON, STOP THE MUSIC...

This is utter rubbish. Let's try again, shall we?

The CALCANEUS is connected to the femur via
the talus.

The METATARSALS are also connected to the talus.

The PHALANGES are connected to the metatarsals.

This is the foot-anatomy dance!

Erm. OK, that's not quite
as catchy. But at least
this version of the song
is accurate!

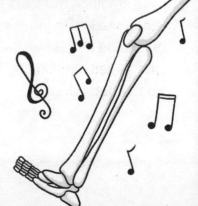

SOPHIE THE STEGOSAURUS

This stegosaurus lived around 100 million years ago, lumbering around a subtropical forest in North America. The scientists who discovered her bones in 2003 were immediately given an important job to do.
And what was that job? To name her, of course! They called her Sophie!

Next, they worked out how she moved by examining her skeleton, and how she ate—by studying her jaw. By measuring Sophie's skull, they could also estimate how big her brain was*. Mind-blowing!

*Sophie's brain was about the size of a walnut, which is pretty tiny considering she weighed around 1.7 tons!

I CAN DEAL WITH THIS · NOT COOL DUDE! · GET AWAY FROM ME! · I'M GOING TO PUKE!

GROSSOMETER

HOW GROSS IS THAT?

CHAPTER 4

SUPER SKIN

Your **SKIN** is the **LARGEST ORGAN** in your body, wrapping you in a waterproof packet. Like cling film, but better! Have you noticed how you never absorb your bathwater? You can thank your skin for that.

This wonderfully waterproof (and germproof) barrier **PROTECTS** and **SHIELDS** everything inside your body. We can **FEEL** using our **SENSE OF TOUCH**, all thanks to touch sensors in our skin. It's also important in helping us **MAINTAIN** our **BODY TEMPERATURE**, by releasing sweat to cool us down, or telling our brain that we need to shiver to help warm us up!

THROUGH THICK AND SKIN

Skin, along with hair and nails, form their own unique body system. Did you know that hair and nails are dead skin cells? It's true. So yes, you're part zombie. But you knew that already.

The skin is made of skin cells—and there are a lot of them. Around **1.6 TRILLION!** Skin cells replicate by the millions every hour, replacing millions of old ones. And where do the old ones go? Well, you shed them in a rather disgusting cloud that follows you around all day.

It's called **DUST**—and it's everywhere...

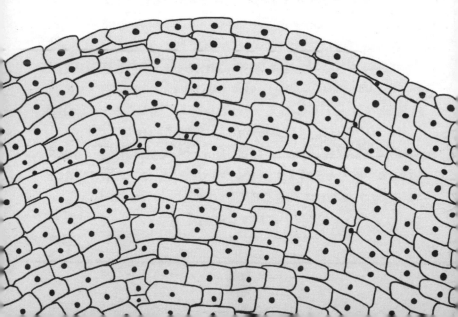

Facts to get under your skin!

☀ Your skin makes up around 16 percent of your whole body.

☀ Your skin is thickest on the soles of your feet, and thinnest on your eyelids!

☀ Your skin sheds around 40,000 skin cells every hour! That's a lot of dust!

☀ Your skin is home to more than 1,000 species of bacteria!

☀ When you're in the bath for a long time, the dead cells on your digits absorb water. This causes the surface area to swell so our body compensates by wrinkling our fingers and toes!

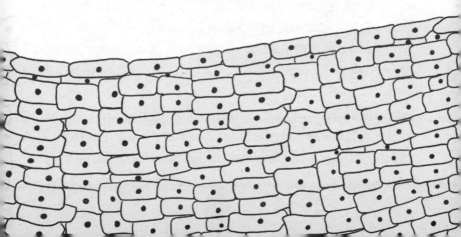

CAKE OF HORRORS

The skin is made up of three main layers—sort of like a disgusting layer cake:

- ✹ On the outside you have the epidermis, a thin protective covering made mostly of dead, scaly cells.

- ✹ Next is the dermis, which is rich with blood vessels and nerve endings.

- ✹ Finally, there's a fat layer supporting the dermis. Hair grows from follicles, which are deep pits within the skin's surface.

EPIDERMIS: this is the top layer. This keeps you waterproof and also gives you your skin colour, depending on the levels of melanin in your epidermis. For example, if you're Black, you have higher levels of melanin in your epidermis than if you're caucasian.

DERMIS: the second layer is the thickest layer, filled with blood vessels, glands, nerves, and touch sensors. This layer includes a sub-layer, called the "finger layer". This is a series of ridges that give us our unique fingerprints!

FAT LAYER: this is the foundation of the skin-house, and has a role in keeping you warm. If we have too much fat in our bodies, this layer gets thicker.

HAIR FOLLICLE: hair grows out of these pockets in the skin.

SWEAT GLAND: these coiled glands ooze liquid that moves to the skin's surface and out through a sweat pore, helping to regulate our body temperature.

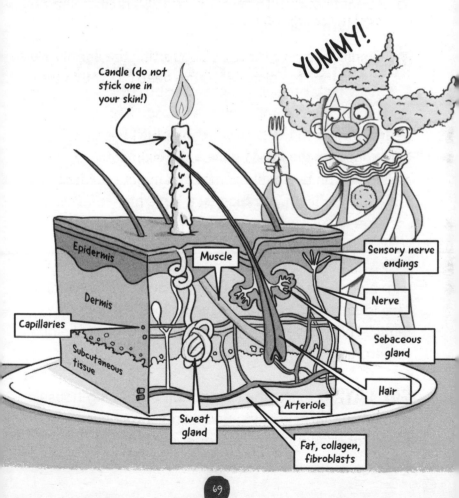

FABULOUS FINGERPRINTS!

A fingerprint is an impression left by the ridges of our fingers. By rolling our finger in ink, then placing our finger on plain paper, we can leave a picture of our finger ridges.

Fingerprints can be used by police to help solve crimes. Print your fingerprints onto the page using ink. See what patterns you have!

HOW TO TAKE YOUR OWN FINGERPRINTS

Put some water-based ink or water-based dark colored paint onto a small sponge. Press your fingers into the sponge, then press them carefully onto the form below.

FINGERPRINT FORM

Name_____

LEFT HAND

1. Little finger	2. Ring finger	3. Middle finger	4. Index finger	5. Thumb

TERRIBLE TWIN

Did you know that identical twins have slightly different fingerprints? Identical twins may have the same DNA, but they often have slightly different physical appearances.

As fingerprints are formed due to the fold in our dermis, they don't turn out the same. So if a twin commits a crime, the police may not be able to solve it based on DNA evidence alone. Let's hope they forgot to wear gloves so there are prints to help convict them!

Age_____   Date_____

RIGHT HAND

1. Thumb	2. Index finger	3. Middle finger	4. Ring finger	5. Little finger

IT MUST HAVE SKIN LOVE

Your skin looks after you. Here are some of the ways that our lovely skin cares for us!

PROTECTION: Our skin is the first line of defense against pathogens. These are organisms that can cause an infection if they get inside you, such as bacteria, viruses, parasites, or fungi.

REGULATION: Our bodies maintain themselves by a process called homeostasis. One important job of the skin is to let your brain know if you're boiling, freezing, or something in between. Bodies need to stay at a balmy 98.6 degrees Fahrenheit. Any higher, and our proteins begin to denature, or break down. If you're too hot then your brain instructs your sweat glands to switch on, releasing sweat and cooling the outer surface of the skin. If you're chilly, your body may shiver—to help warm you up!

TOUCH: Without this sense, you wouldn't be able to feel your cat's soft fur, or experience sea water sloshing over your toes at the seaside. The skin has touch receptors that link to our nervous system, sending signals hurtling to the brain.

HAIR AND NAILS

Unlike most other warm-blooded animals, we humans have lost most of our body hair. Bare skin probably evolved to help us deal with warmer temperatures. But as humans moved around the world to colder regions, they needed to put on extra layers. So, that's when we invented clothes!

HAIRY HORNS

Hair and nails are actually dead skin cells. They're made of a protein called keratin. Rhino horn is also made of keratin, as are some animal hooves!

Many cultures believe that rhino horns have medicinal properties, although there is little scientific evidence to support this. Rhinos are often hunted for their horns, which has led them to the edge of extinction. Let's leave the rhinos alone, shall we?

TOOT!

BUMPS, BRUISES, SCRATCHES, & SCABS!

Sometimes, you bump yourself and a bruise appears on your skin. This is where blood vessels in the dermis leak due to the impact, causing a flow of blood into the surrounding area. Luckily, most bruises aren't too serious. They clear up in a few days.

If you're unlucky enough to scratch or cut yourself, you'll probably see some blood come out, which will eventually turn into a scab. A scab is a crusty lump of blood and sebum that forms over a wound, healing the hole. **DON'T PICK IT!**

Q: What's the number one cause of dry skin?

A: Towels!

OUCH!

PIMPLES AND PUS

Everyone has pimples at some time in their life. No one likes them, especially when they appear the night before you're going to your best friend's birthday party! Pimples form when oil glands in your skin get clogged up. Instead of moisturizing the skin, they bubble up with oil and dead skin cells. They become what we call blackheads or whiteheads. Whiteheads are my favorite. They're the ones that POP, sending pus all over your bathroom mirror!

Q: What do you need to get rid of a demon with a skin condition?

A: An Exorcyst.

CREEPY CRAWLIES

You share your skin with lots of creepy-crawlies. They're on you, right now. Can you feel them tickling your face? No? Well, they're definitely there. Most of them are completely normal. They're called *Demodex*, also known as eyelash mites. Yes, they're on your eyelashes right now. Sorry.

You may not want eyelash mites on you, but they're so small I bet you didn't even notice. Sometimes we get infested with much larger critters, such as...body lice!

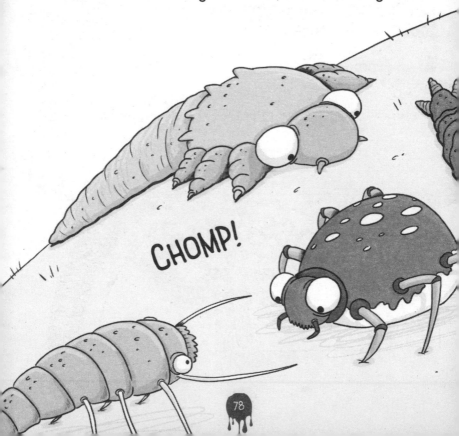

CHOMP!

An infestation of body lice happens when we touch infected clothing, or brush heads with an infected person. Lice are parasitic insects that feed on human blood, and can infest the head and body!

MUNCH!

GROSSOMETER
HOW GROSS IS THAT?

I CAN DEAL WITH THIS
NOT COOL DUDE!
GET AWAY FROM ME!
I'M GOING TO PUKE!

SKINNED ALIVE

The first documented case of someone being skinned alive was in around 800 BC. It was practiced by the ancient Aztecs as part of their sacrificial rituals to their gods, and used as a form of punishment in medieval Europe. Fortunately, "flaying" (its proper name) doesn't happen so much these days. As it's incredibly painful, this would have been a hideous way to go.

Let's try to forget the flaying, shall we...

It's time to focus on something a little less gross for a moment. Our **SENSATIONAL SENSES**!

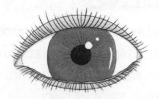

CHAPTER 5

SENSATIONAL SENSES

These five senses allow us to
DISCOVER, EXPERIENCE, and **UNDERSTAND**
the world around us.

Without them, we wouldn't be able to see the
colors of a rainbow or hear bird song in the
morning. We wouldn't smell the scent of cherry
blossom in spring or taste the delicious flavors
of ice cream. And, perhaps most importantly, we
wouldn't feel the touch of a loved one as they put
their arms around us to give us a
MASSIVE CUDDLE!

EVERYDAY GREATNESS

Not everyone is able to use all five of their senses. Blind people are unable to see, while deaf people are unable to hear. Some people with paralysis are unable to feel parts of their body.

This different way of being can bring challenges, but it also allows for unique lives that can inspire others:

- The Paralympics began in 1960 with eight sports—today it has nearly 30 different sports.

- In 2001, Erik W. Weihenmayer became the first blind man to reach the summit of Mount Everest.

- The deaf actress Rose Ayling-Ellis won the British TV dance competion Strictly Come Dancing in 2021 (see page 201). After her success, there was a surge of people learning sign language.

AND

- Someone you know has probably lost their sense of smell or taste for a while! Why? Because millions of people around the world discovered that they'd lost these senses as a symptom of COVID-19. These senses returned for most people when they recovered.

IT ALL MAKES SENSE NOW!

Our senses work thanks to these outstanding organs:

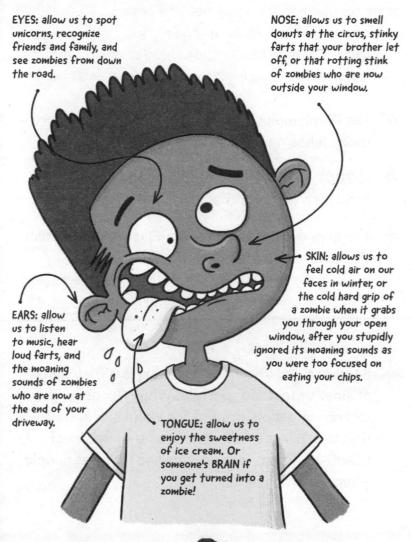

EYES: allow us to spot unicorns, recognize friends and family, and see zombies from down the road.

NOSE: allows us to smell donuts at the circus, stinky farts that your brother let off, or that rotting stink of zombies who are now outside your window.

SKIN: allows us to feel cold air on our faces in winter, or the cold hard grip of a zombie when it grabs you through your open window, after you stupidly ignored its moaning sounds as you were too focused on eating your chips.

EARS: allow us to listen to music, hear loud farts, and the moaning sounds of zombies who are now at the end of your driveway.

TONGUE: allow us to enjoy the sweetness of ice cream. Or someone's BRAIN if you get turned into a zombie!

EYE, EYE, CAPTAIN!

Eyes are not only beautiful, but they're amazing too. They have millions of special cells that work by detecting light. This allows them to collect vast amounts of visual information. The brain converts this data into 3D images of the world around us.

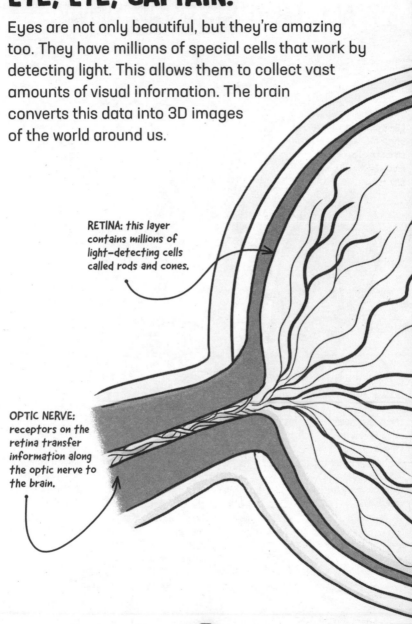

RETINA: this layer contains millions of light-detecting cells called rods and cones.

OPTIC NERVE: receptors on the retina transfer information along the optic nerve to the brain.

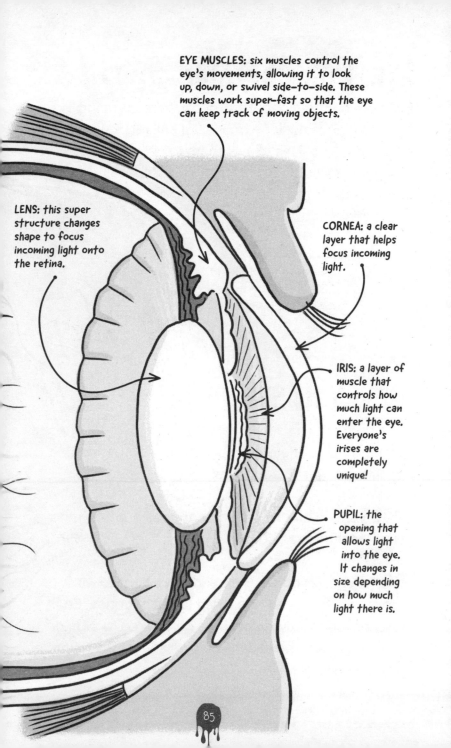

EYE MUSCLES: six muscles control the eye's movements, allowing it to look up, down, or swivel side-to-side. These muscles work super-fast so that the eye can keep track of moving objects.

LENS: this super structure changes shape to focus incoming light onto the retina.

CORNEA: a clear layer that helps focus incoming light.

IRIS: a layer of muscle that controls how much light can enter the eye. Everyone's irises are completely unique!

PUPIL: the opening that allows light into the eye. It changes in size depending on how much light there is.

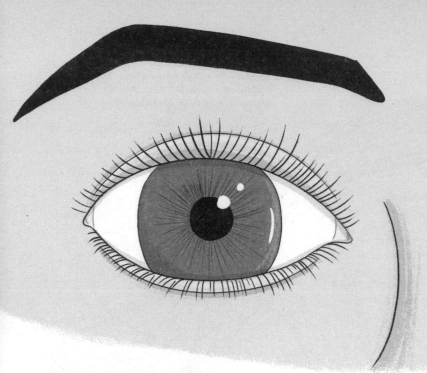

HOW YOU SEE

The retina uses special cells called rods and cones to process light. There are about 100 million rods and 7 million cones in each eye!

RODS see in black and white and tell our brain the shapes of things.

CONES see in color, and need more light to work properly. The retina has three types of cones. Each type can identify one of three colors: red, green, or blue. Together, these cells help us see all the colors of the rainbow!

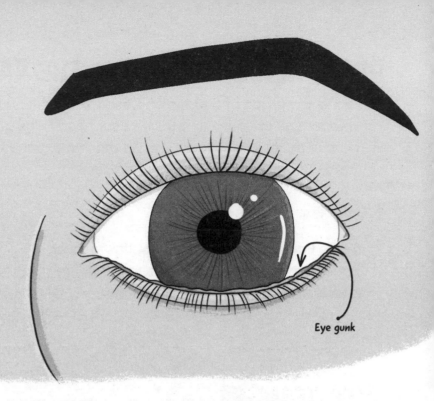

Eye gunk

People with color blindness have problems with some of their cones, which affects their ability to see red and green.

HELPFUL EYE GUNK

Our eyes produce a type of mucus called rheum. Rheum protects the eyes from dirt, pollution, and foreign materials. The eyes release rheum to catch any unwanted dust or dirt and collect it into neat little blobs. When rheum leaves the eyeball and dries up, it can leave behind eye gunk. Some people call this "sleep" as these secretions often continue at nighttime, so you wake up to find eye gunk! It may be gross, but it's super helpful!

HEAR, HEAR! ALL ABOUT THE EAR

The ear is the organ of hearing and balance, but did you know that most of your ear is inside your head? The outer skin flap is the only visible part, while the rest expands out inside your skull! It has three main parts:

1. Outer Ear: collects sound!

2. Middle Ear: where elves fight goblins—oh wait— that's Middle-earth! The Middle Ear is where sounds are converted into vibrations.

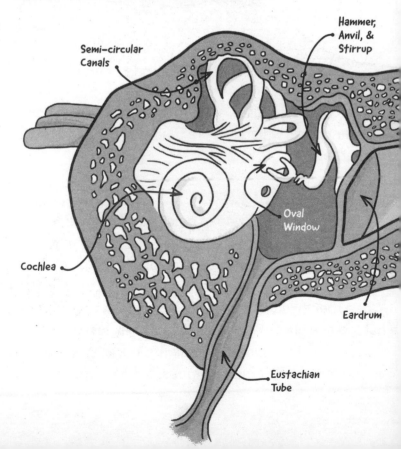

Semi-circular Canals

Hammer, Anvil, & Stirrup

Oval Window

Cochlea

Eardrum

Eustachian Tube

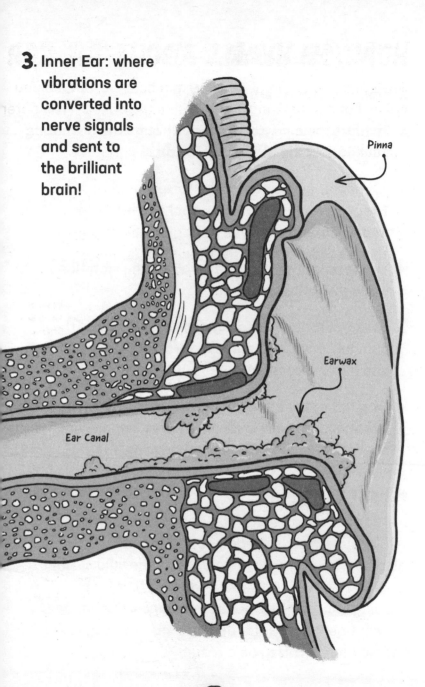

3. Inner Ear: where vibrations are converted into nerve signals and sent to the brilliant brain!

Pinna

Earwax

Ear Canal

HOW YOU HEAR

1. Someone rips a very loud FART!

2. The farty sound-waves travel through the air, hitting your ears at the SPEED OF SOUND!

3. Your outer ear captures the farty sound waves. They travel along the ear canal and hit the ear drum with a TOOT!

4. The eardrum vibrates, generating tiny vibrations throughout the inner ear.

5. These vibrations pass over three tiny bones (the hammer, anvil, and stirrup), through the oval window, and into the cochlea.

6. Tiny hairs inside the cochlea pick up the farty vibrations, convert them into nerve signals, and send them to the brain for processing!

PERFECT BALANCE

Our ears are also essential for our balance. The semicircular canals inside your ear contain three fluid-filled tubes. As you move your body, the fluid sloshes around. This sloshing sends signals to the brain, allowing your body to maintain balance. Sometimes, when we get an ear infection, the signals go haywire, and we can feel dizzy as a result!

Eardrum-Bursting Blast

In 1883, the volcanic eruption of Krakatoa in Indonesia caused permanent hearing loss to people who were up to ONE HUNDRED MILES AWAY at the time of the explosion. It's impossible to imagine how loud the eruption must have been to make this happen!

SMELL YOU LATER!

Molecules in the air float up our nose, tickle our nasal receptors, and send signals to the brain. Some things, like roses, smell like roses. Some things, however, smell disgusting—like rotting zombies or big piles of poop. We naturally dislike stinky stuff. This is an evolutionary trick to keep us away from danger—like bacteria in poop (or rotting zombies who want to steal your chips.)

MARVELOUS MUCUS

Mucus is a sticky, gloopy bodily secretion, and it comes in many different colors: yellows, browns, and greens. SNOT is the name we give to mucus from the nose (nasal mucus). It's your first line of defense against bacteria, viruses, dust, and pollen, which could all affect your breathing if they reached the lungs. Snot helps to trap all this stuff, keeping your airways clear. Tiny hairs inside your nose called cilia (SIL-ee-ah) help move the snot out of your nose and toward your nostrils.

BOOGER BONANZA

Once snot reaches the end of your nozzle, it dries into crumbly little **BOOGERS.** These come in many shapes and sizes. Some are slimy and squishy, and others are crumbly and dry. Most people blow their boogers into tissues, but gross people do something else entirely. It's called...

Rhinotillexis—the scientific word for **PICKING YOUR NOSE!**

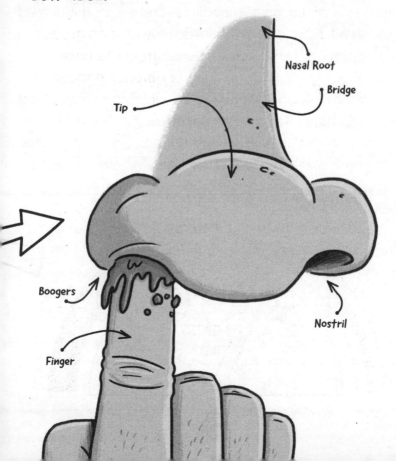

TANTALIZING TASTE

The tongue has thousands of taste buds on its surface, allowing us to taste a variety of different flavors. But amazingly, they all fall into one of five types.

Can you match the five taste types below with the correct food?

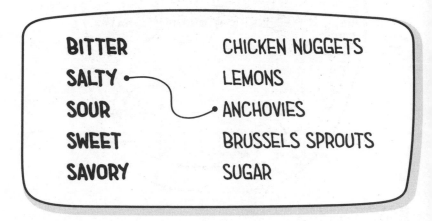

BITTER   CHICKEN NUGGETS
SALTY   LEMONS
SOUR   ANCHOVIES
SWEET   BRUSSELS SPROUTS
SAVORY   SUGAR

PLAQUE ATTACK!

Brush your teeth twice a day for about two minutes, otherwise you'll be prone to a **PLAQUE ATTACK**! Plaque is a film of bacteria that forms on the surfaces of your teeth. These bacteria go into overdrive after you eat or drink, producing acid that can damage your tooth enamel, cause holes (cavities) or even damage your gums (gingivitis)! Just remember the rule of two by two —twice a day, for two minutes.

Answers: Bitter = Brussels sprouts, Salty = Anchovies, Sour = Lemons, Sweet = Sugar, Savory = Chicken nuggets

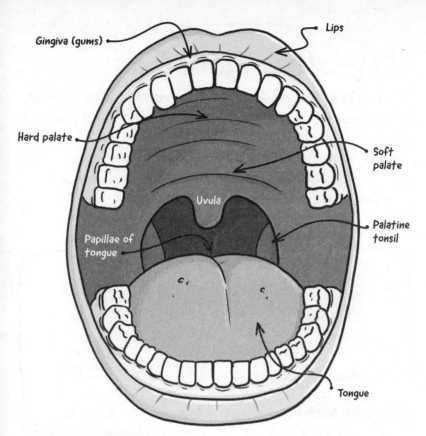

Gingiva (gums)

Lips

Hard palate

Soft palate

Uvula

Palatine tonsil

Papillae of tongue

Tongue

GASSY GUMS

Halitosis is the scientific word for bad breath. It can come from eating strong-smelling foods or from problems with your teeth or gums. Unfortunately for some people, brushing is not always enough! Sometimes if food builds up between your teeth it can form lumps of foul-smelling gunk that can make your breath smell like a sewer! If you ever find your mouth is stinky even after you brush, you may need to floss and remove the stuff between your teeth, too. But always check with your dentist first—they're there to help!

Sense-ational Facts

Can you guess how many of the below fantastic facts are true?

✳ Your nasal membranes produce nearly two gallons of mucus each week, but you swallow most of it without even realizing!

⸬ All people with blue eyes have one common ancestor.

⸬ The shape of your nose affects the sound of your voice.

⸬ Your eye muscles move more than 100,000 times every day.

⸬ Your pupils get bigger when you focus on your homework.

⸬ Your voice sounds lower to you than it does to the people around you.

✳ Your nose can smell more odors than there are people on Earth.

⸬ Every thirty minutes you blink more times than there are days in the year!

⸬ If your vision was as good as a golden eagle's, you could stand on the top of a roller coaster and still see a ladybug on the ground.

Answer: THEY'RE ALL TRUE!

CHAPTER 6

YOU'RE ALL HEART

The HEART is the ENGINE of your FANTASTIC BODY.

The amazing heart contracts and relaxes around seventy times every minute. This regular rhythm pumps blood around the body. After it squeezes out blood, it quickly fills up again, ready for the next beat. This engine is very important. Without it, you wouldn't be able to survive!

THE MIGHTY MUSCLE

Your heart started working well before you were even born, when you were a tiny embryo in your mother's womb. And your heart will continue to beat throughout your entire life. It never takes any time off.

To keep the heart beating, the cardiac muscle cells need a constant supply of:

1. Fuel   **2.** Oxygen

These are delivered by the coronary blood supply. This network of blood vessels is specific to the heart. It branches through the heart's wall to reach all parts of the mighty muscle. It's important that blood can always reach everywhere in the heart and, eventually, the body.

WHERE IS YOUR HEART?

This cone-shaped muscle is located inside the chest (thorax), protected by the rib cage. It sits slightly to the left of your breastbone (sternum) and between your two lungs.

HOW LEFT IS LEFT?

The heart doesn't sit as far to the left of your body as you might think, but because the left-hand ventricle pumps strongly it feels as though the heart is more to the left of your chest. This means that when people take a pledge by putting their right hand over their left chest, they aren't really swearing on their heart at all. They're swearing on their left lung!

BLOOD SUPERHIGHWAY

Circulation is the name for a process where the heart pumps blood around the body through millions of blood vessels—or tubes, all of different sizes. If you removed someone's blood vessels and lined them up, end to end, they'd be very annoyed with you. They'd also discover that their vessels reach over 100,000 miles—enough to go around Planet Earth four times!

Blood vessels deliver oxygen and other essential nutrients to the body's cells and tissues. There are three types in the body:

1. Arteries   **2**. Veins   **3**. Capillaries

ARTERIES carry blood rich with oxygen away from the heart to other places.

VEINS carry blood low in oxygen back to the heart.

CAPILLARIES are a vast network of tiny blood vessels. They're so thin they allow oxygen to move out into the tissues and carbon dioxide to move in, so it can be removed from the body.

INSIDE THE HEART

Ever wonder what goes on inside your heart? It's a complicated pump which takes blood in and pushes it out again, all around your body.

AORTA: the body's largest artery that transports blood from the heart to the body

VENA CAVA: a large vein that delivers blood to the heart from the body

PULMONARY VEIN: brings blood back from the lungs

A Hearty Size

★ A new-born baby's heart is the size of a table tennis ball.

★ A healthy adult's heart is the size of a clenched fist.

★ The fairy fly, a type of wasp, has the smallest heart in the world!

★ The blue whale has the largest heart in the world!

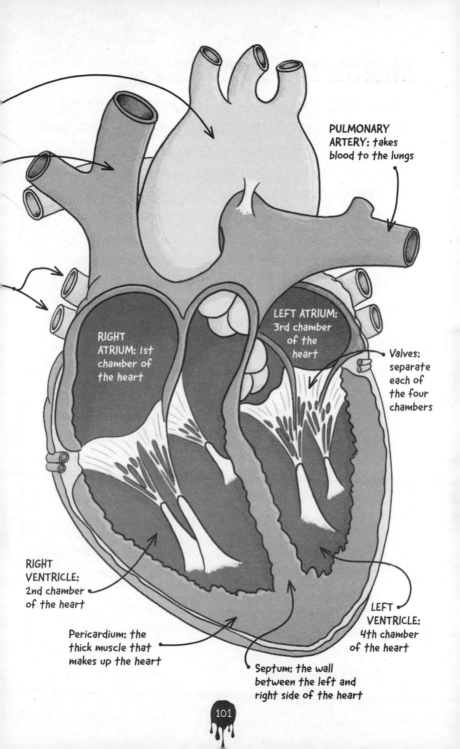

PULMONARY ARTERY: takes blood to the lungs

RIGHT ATRIUM: 1st chamber of the heart

LEFT ATRIUM: 3rd chamber of the heart

Valves: separate each of the four chambers

RIGHT VENTRICLE: 2nd chamber of the heart

LEFT VENTRICLE: 4th chamber of the heart

Pericardium: the thick muscle that makes up the heart

Septum: the wall between the left and right side of the heart

HOW THE HEART WORKS

A single heartbeat only lasts a second. But a lot happens during this short time!

Our heart's rhythm is controlled by something called the **sinus node**, located inside the wall of the right atrium.

The sinus node is sometimes called the heart's natural pacemaker. It generates electrical signals that move outward in a wave across the heart, making the heart's chambers contract at different times to move blood to different places at exactly the right time.

Did you know?

There are valves in between each of the heart's chambers. The LUP-DUP sound of a heartbeat is made by the different valves closing!

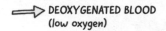 **DEOXYGENATED BLOOD**
(low oxygen)

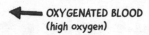 **OXYGENATED BLOOD**
(high oxygen)

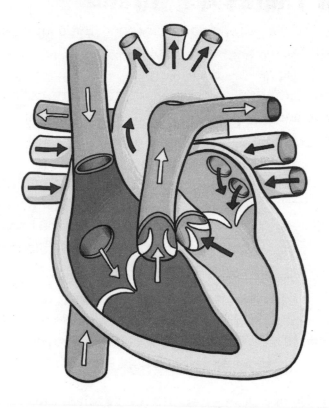

1. Blood arrives: the heart muscle relaxes, and blood enters the upper left and right heart chambers (atria).

2. Atria to ventricles: the two atria contract and blood flows into the chambers below (ventricles).

3. Blood leaves: lastly, the ventricles contract and force blood either to the lungs or to the rest of the body.

DON'T MISS A BEAT

In certain places on the body, you can feel your pulse: the little thump each heartbeat makes. The easiest place to feel your pulse is on your wrist.

To find your wrist pulse, place two fingers from your other hand against the base of your thumb, and then drag them down to the inner wrist. Try to find it now! Did you feel your pulse? Hooray, you are alive!

Top Tip

Don't use your thumb to feel your wrist pulse... because your thumb has a tiny pulse in it, too! This will only confuse you if you try to count your BPM. And what's your BPM...?

FYI, BPM

BPM stands for Beats Per Minute. So 60 Beats Per Minute is one heartbeat per second! Exercise makes the heart rate go up—but strong emotions like stress, fear, or excitement can change your heartbeat. When you sleep or relax, your heartbeat slows down.

BPM CHART

A person's average resting heart rate depends on factors such as their age, gender, and level of fitness.

(And whether they're alive!)

Zombie: 0 bpm

Baby: 120 bpm

10-year-old: 90 bpm

Woman: 78 bpm

Man: 70 bpm

American Pygmy Shrew: 1,200 bpm

(one of the smallest mammals in the world, with the fastest heartbeat in the world!)

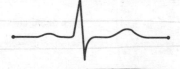

ALL ABOUT BLOOD

Blood circulates throughout all parts of our terrific tissues, keeping them fueled with important nutrients and oxygen. Blood is a liquid tissue made up of trillions of cells floating in a watery substance called plasma. Blood also transports waste products to be discarded from our bodies.

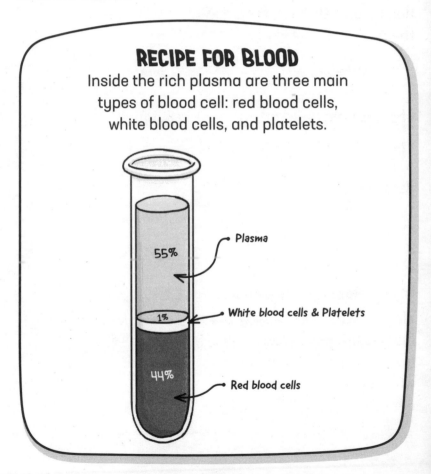

RECIPE FOR BLOOD

Inside the rich plasma are three main types of blood cell: red blood cells, white blood cells, and platelets.

55% • Plasma

1% • White blood cells & Platelets

44% • Red blood cells

RED BLOOD CELLS contain a protein called hemoglobin. Oxygen enters our bodies through the lungs and is picked up by hemoglobin, to be carried around the body to our tissues. Hemoglobin is what gives our blood its red color! The more hemoglobin there is, the brighter the red!

WHITE BLOOD CELLS are important cells that form part of our immune system—our body's defenses.

PLATELETS are important for clotting. They act as tiny building blocks that clump together, blocking up wounds and helping us heal. Like when we scratch ourselves or have our arm bitten by a zombie...

CHANGE OF HEART

The science of the heart is called cardiology, and doctors who look after people's heart health are cardiologists.

The first open-heart surgery was completed by Dr. Daniel Hale Williams in 1893. Daniel was one of the world's first Black cardiologists.

Daniel Hale Williams

The first human heart transplant (that worked) was done by Dr. Christiaan Barnard at the Groote Schuur Hospital in Cape Town, South Africa in 1967. Christiaan operated on Louis Washkansky, who was terminally ill with heart failure. Heart failure is when the heart is no longer able to pump blood properly around the body.

Dr. Christiaan Barnard

Barnard's team replaced Louis's damaged heart with that of a donor. The donor, Denise Darvall, was only twenty-five when she died in a car accident. Denise's dad knew she would have wanted to help others, so he agreed for her organs to be donated. Since then, heart transplants have been done all around the world!

CARDIOLOGY QUIZ

QUESTION 1
How many chambers does the heart have?

- [ ] a. Three
- [ ] b. Four
- [ ] c. Five
- [ ] d. Six

QUESTION 2
The wall that separates the left and right sides of the heart is called the:

- [ ] a. Great Wall of China
- [ ] b. Atrium
- [ ] c. Ventricle
- [ ] d. Septum

TURN THE PAGE
UPSIDE DOWN TO SEE
THE ANSWERS!

Answers: 1b, 2d, 3c, 4b, 5b

QUESTION 3

The movement of blood through the body's circulation is called:

- ☐ a. Heart Pumping
- ☐ b. Locomotion
- ☐ c. Circulation
- ☐ d. Farting

QUESTION 4

The beating sound your heart makes comes from:

- ☐ a. Blood going in the wrong direction
- ☐ b. Valves closing
- ☐ c. The heart skipping a beat
- ☐ d. Heart cells practicing with their drum kit

QUESTION 5

The tubes that carry blood back to your heart are called:

- ☐ a. Arteries
- ☐ b. Veins
- ☐ c. Pipes
- ☐ d. Bananas

Heart Facts

* Your heart beats around 115,000 times a day, or 2.5 billion times in a lifetime!

* Water makes up about 75 percent of the heart's weight.

* There are five million red blood cells in every drop of human blood.

* Your heart pumps over 2,000 gallons of blood around the body each day. That's enough to fill this wading pool!

I CAN DEAL WITH THIS · NOT COOL DUDE! · GET AWAY FROM ME! · I'M GOING TO PUKE!

GROSSOMETER

HOW GROSS IS THAT?

CHAPTER 7

LOVELY LUNGS

The **LUNGS** are our **BREATHING** organs.
Their job is to get oxygen into our
bloodstream and get waste gases out.

When we **BREATHE IN** air through our nose
and mouth, we are nourished with **OXYGEN**
that goes into our airways.

When we **BREATHE OUT**, we push out air
containing **CARBON DIOXIDE**.

But we also use breathing for other things, such as...

blowing out the candles
on a birthday cake

WHOOSH!

playing musical
instruments, such as
recorders or flutes,
that rely on circular
breathing

singing, which also needs
us to breathe in and out

FA LA LA LA LA!

BEST FRIENDS FOREVER

The lungs and heart are best friends. They have a unique and important relationship. The heart pumps blood to the lungs so that it can pick up oxygen, sending it on a long journey through the circulatory system to our tissues. The cells throughout our fabulous body use this oxygen to release energy, and this process creates carbon dioxide. The carbon dioxide is picked up and returned to the lungs, where we breathe it out into the world.

PLANT A TREE

Plants produce oxygen thanks to a process called photosynthesis. They need carbon dioxide to do this. So, while we breathe out carbon dioxide, plants pick it up. And when plants release oxygen, we—and the rest of the animal kingdom—breathe it in. Doesn't that make you want to become best friends with a tree?

What Is Circular Breathing?

It is a way of keeping the breath moving through our body...all the time! As we breathe in, we can also breathe out—this keeps air moving through our mouth, throat, and lungs!

BREATHE IN, BREATHE OUT

When the lungs breathe in air, they expand (grow in size). They are surrounded by muscles that help them do this. The diaphragm is one of the most important muscles needed for breathing. When the lungs breathe out, the muscles relax and the lungs get smaller.

LEARN ABOUT LUNGS

Lungs have a pinkish color thanks to their large network of capillaries. A capillary is a large, branching blood vessel—a bit like the branches on a tree. These carry blood supply around the lungs. There's...

✳ ...a trunk, called the TRACHEA. Next, there are two large branches...

✳ ...called BRONCHI. These branch out into many twigs called BRONCHIOLES.

✳ The "leaves" on the tree are tiny and are called ALVEOLI.

BREATHING RATES

The rate of our breathing changes depending on what we're doing:

- Sitting quietly / meditating: 15 breaths per minute

- Walking the dog: 20 breaths per minute

- Running in the park: 40 breaths per minute

- Running away from a zombie: 60–70 breaths per minute!

INSIDE STORY

The lungs are surrounded by two slimy membranes called pleurae. There's a thin layer of liquid between them, allowing them to slide over each other. This means the lungs can expand and shrink as we breathe in and out.

TRACHEA: Also known as the windpipe—where air flows from the mouth and nose to the lungs.

BRONCHUS: The trachea branches into two bronchi (one is called a bronchus).

BRONCHIOLES: The two bronchi branch further into many bronchioles.

ALVEOLI: The "leaves of the tree," these are microscopic air bags covered in capillaries. This is where gas exchange happens: picking up oxygen and dropping off carbon dioxide.

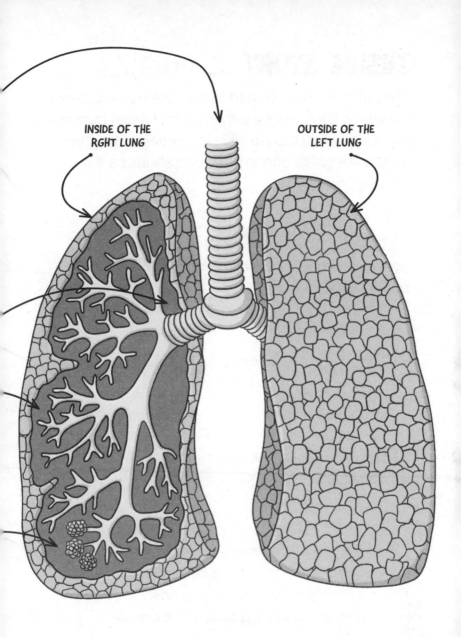

INSIDE OF THE RGHT LUNG

OUTSIDE OF THE LEFT LUNG

LIGHTS, CAMERA, ALVEOLI!

At the end of the bronchioles are a bunch of grapes—the alveoli. These bunches can only be seen under a microscope—they're that tiny! So tiny in fact, that around **300,000** alveoli manage to squeeze inside each lung!

LOVE YOUR LUNGS

Our lungs are so important for a healthy life. But they are very delicate and, over time, can be damaged. For example, by breathing in pollution or by smoking. Smoking makes the normally pink lungs turn black from a buildup of tar. Smoking is bad for us, and tar is even worse. Let's love our lungs instead!

GAS EXCHANGE

Every second of our lives, the life-sustaining process of gas exchange happens. Gas exchange is the name scientists give to how oxygen enters the bloodstream and carbon dioxide leaves.

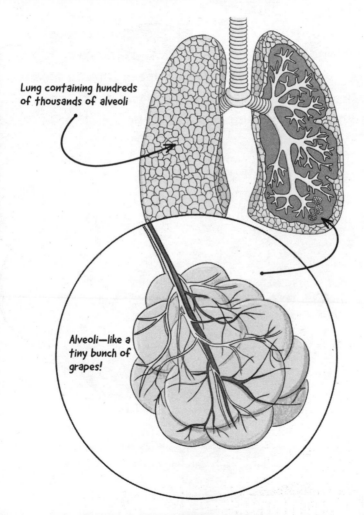

Lung containing hundreds of thousands of alveoli

Alveoli—like a tiny bunch of grapes!

SAY IT, SING IT, SHOUT IT!

Humans are social creatures. Speech is an important part of our lives and society. It's what makes us unique in the animal kingdom and is closely linked to our breathing.

As we breathe air out, it passes through an awesome organ called the larynx—also known as the voice box. The larynx is located at the back of our throats next to where our tongues finish. There are two membranes stretched across the larynx, called the vocal cords.

When we speak, muscles pull the vocal cords together and air moves through the small gap. The vocal cords vibrate and make sounds. The different sounds we make when we speak, sing, or shout are changed by the ways our tongues, mouths, and lips move. Amazing, really!

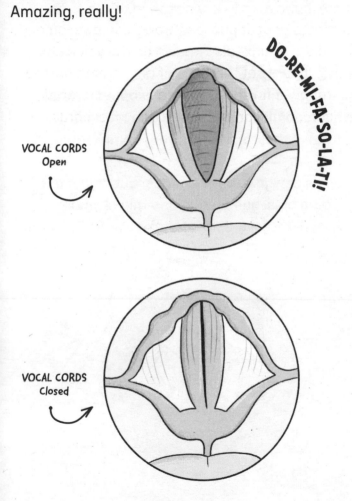

DO-RE-MI-FA-SO-LA-TI!

VOCAL CORDS
Open

VOCAL CORDS
Closed

HUMAN SPEECH

Scientists believe that our ancestors may have developed the ability to make certain sounds around 25 million years ago. But language as we know it today probably only developed around 300,000 years ago (a long time, but a drop in the ocean in terms of our evolution).

SING LIKE A WHALE

Speaking of oceans, have you ever listened to whale song? It's beautiful, and the way these magnificent creatures make these sounds is very complicated.

Many species of whale make sounds, but only a few sing, including blue, humpback, and minke whales. Scientists have discovered that these species of whale

have folds in their voice boxes, very similar in structure to our own. Like in humans, those cords vibrate as air flows over them, producing different sounds.

What makes whales different, though, is the way they can still make sounds even while underwater. Their unique voice boxes means that they can still make sounds without losing any air. Incredible!

STRANGE SOUNDS

Normal breathing happens in a regular rhythm. But sometimes, there's an interruption to this regular flow, and strange things can happen!

COUGHS: if your body needs to clear something in your airway, your brain sends a signal to cough.

HICCUPS: sometimes the nerves around the diaphragm fire off incorrectly, making it jerk. These are known as hiccups!

SNEEZES: if something gets in your nose, your brain sends a signal to expel it by blowing it out!

AAAH-CHOO!

SNORES: our vocal cords relax when we sleep, and sometimes this means the air flowing over them can make loud noises. VERY loud, in your dad's case!

YAWNS: this is when you take a very deep breath with your mouth wide open. I bet you're yawning just thinking about it!

YAAAA-AAWN!

A Different Kind of Breath

Not all animals breathe like us. In fact, there are four different ways that animals breathe!

1. WITH LUNGS: Mammals, birds, reptiles, and some amphibians.

2. WITH GILLS: Fish and crabs (water flows in, and gas exchange happens directly via the gills).

3. WITH A TRACHEA (WINDPIPE): Insects, spiders, and centipedes.

4. And...wait for it...with SKIN! Most amphibians.

TOAD-ALLY AMAZING!

Some animals transform so much, they even change the way they breathe!

* Tadpoles have gills, but when they change into froglets, their respiratory system changes too!

* Their gills disappear as they go through metamorphosis (this means "change").

* And, finally, once they're an adult frog, they use their lungs and skin to breathe instead!

GILLS TODAY, LUNGS TOMORROW!

CHAPTER 8

AMAZING ABDOMEN

Many of the body's most important organs are inside a large space that sits between your chest and your pelvis called the **ABDOMEN**.

This amazing area holds your **DIGESTIVE** and **URINARY SYSTEMS** and your **REPRODUCTIVE ORGANS** too.

Your abdomen is where one of the grossest secretions in the whole body is made: **BILE!** This **SLIMY SUBSTANCE** can give your **PUKE** a greeny-yellow tinge when you're sick— and it stinks really bad too! **YUCK!**

PLAY THE NAME GAME

Are you ready to play the name game? It's not for the faint-hearted!

Which of these organs exist inside the abdomen? All the names are listed in alphabetical order, but only **NINE** answers are right! Can you spot the right labels for real parts of the body?

TURN THE PAGE
UPSIDE DOWN TO SEE
THE ANSWERS!

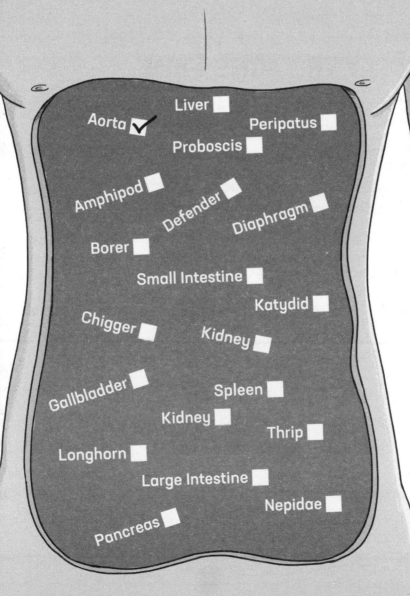

KEEP YOURSELF TOGETHER!

How does the abdomen keep all these parts together?
Why don't they all just float around the body?

That's due to connective tissues called mesentery.
They allow the body parts to move and squish about,
and even slide up against each other.

BUT HOW?

Mesentery is made up of several connected cells. They
attach your organs to a body wall and stop everything
from collapsing into your pelvis. Good job!

OTHERWISE, YOU'D LOOK LIKE THIS!

BUSY LIVER

Your liver is BUSY. It has about 500 jobs to perform, including...

★ Removing toxic substances from your blood

★ Storing all those lovely vitamins and minerals you need to keep your body in tip top condition

★ Producing and storing sugar needed for energy

★ Creating bile (more on this juicy goo soon...)

Fascinating Fact!

The liver is the largest gland in the body and the second largest organ (after the skin). An adult's liver weighs around 3.3 lb, which is about the same as ten golden hamsters!

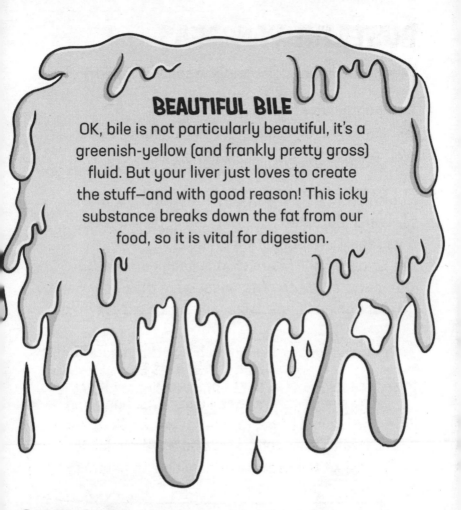

BEAUTIFUL BILE

OK, bile is not particularly beautiful, it's a greenish-yellow (and frankly pretty gross) fluid. But your liver just loves to create the stuff—and with good reason! This icky substance breaks down the fat from our food, so it is vital for digestion.

SUPER LIVER

Livers are basically superheroes and can even regenerate. A person can donate over half their liver to someone else, and their own liver will regrow after just a few months!

POWERFUL PANCREAS

Q: What's long and flat and shaped like a pear?

A: A pear you've just sat on?

Well, maybe. But also...your pancreas!

But isn't that a train station in London? No, that's **ST. PANCRAS!** Which has nothing to do with your pancreas. Or pears, for that matter.

Your pancreas is an organ nestled in the upper part of your abdomen. It has two super-important tasks to do...

1. Produce digestive juices to break down your food.

2. Release hormones (including insulin) to keep the amount of sugar in your blood at the right level.

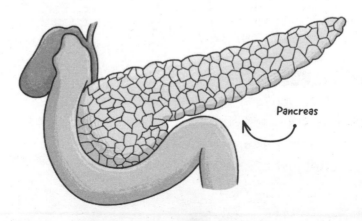

Pancreas

AMAZING APPENDIX

Did you ever imagine that there might be a whole part of your body that **NO ONE UNDERSTANDS?**

That's the appendix...

- **It's the size of a little finger**

- **Human beings are one of the few animals that have one**

- **It grows out of the large intestine**

- **Ancient Egyptians called it the worm of the bowel**

- **Leonardo da Vinci may have drawn the first picture of an appendix**

- **The appendix probably came about because it was needed to help our immune system**

Scientists still can't figure out the job of an appendix, but let's all say "**YEAH!**" for the most mysterious part of our body.

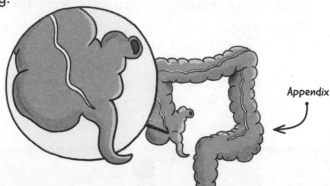

Appendix

KIDNEY MAGIC

Your kidneys are a pair of bean-shaped magicians. These organs remove waste products from blood and transform them into...pee!

Five Fantastic Kidney Numbers...

* Most people are born with **2** kidneys, but we only need one to live.

* Your kidneys filter **45** gallons of blood a day— enough to fill a fish tank!

* **7**—the number of years a woman had added to her life after she was treated with...sausage skins and a wooden drum fixed together, to give her temporary help! This was all thanks to a homemade blood-filtering machine made by Dutch doctor Willem Kolff in 1945.

* An Egyptian papyrus from **3,500** years ago contains the first known description of a kidney!

* Around one in ten thousand people are born with **4** kidneys!

HEAT AND HEALTH

Kidneys are amazingly adaptable, but there's one challenge they can't face—climate change. Soaring temperatures mean that manual workers in some parts of the world, such as Central America and South Asia, have more kidney disease. Why? The extreme heat means that people sweat more than ever, which makes them dehydrated...which leads to kidney disease.

"THIS CAN BE CONSIDERED THE FIRST DISEASE THAT'S RELATED TO CLIMATE CHANGE"

Dr. Roberto Lucchini, Florida International University

139

THE PEE MAP

When you pee, what do you think happens? Here's a map of the most exciting fluid to leave your body. You made this!

When you drink something, it goes into your tummy.

From there, the liquid enters your intestines and blood.

The blood gets filtered by your kidneys.

Any water that the body doesn't need goes to your bladder.

The bladder is like a small balloon! It fills with water.

I Really Need To Pee!

You're not alone. Did you know that most people between eight and twelve years old pee about five to seven times a day? A young person's bladder can hold up to fourteen ounces of pee—two cups of water!

Once this happens, you get an urge to...pee. That means you're controlling science with your own body!

The pee (or urine) goes into a part of your body called the urethra.

You ask for a potty break and...

WEEEEEE!

141

WHAT IS THE URETHRA?

Simple! This is a tube that passes liquid out of the body. A urethra is different depending on whether you're a boy or a girl. The male urethra is approximately four times longer than a female urethra.

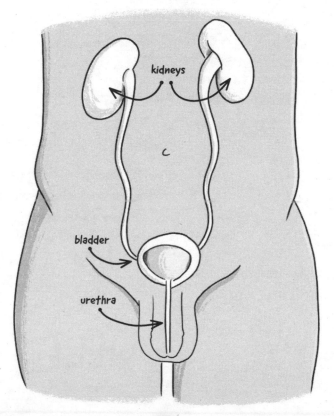

MALE kidneys
and urethra

kidneys

bladder

urethra

For the urethra to do its job, it needs the sphincter muscle to relax...chill out...take it easy. The sphincter is a layer of strong muscles around the bottom of your body. Your brain will pass a message to these parts, instructing them to release liquid.

Brains and bodies. Aren't they amazing?

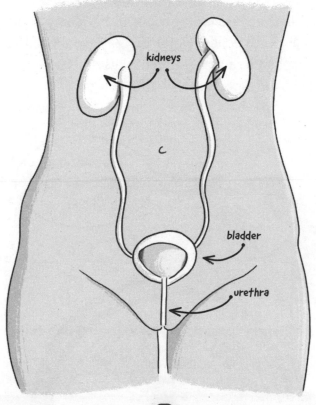

FEMALE kidneys and urethra

kidneys

bladder

urethra

DEALING WITH DIABETES

Diabetes is a condition in which there's too much sugar in the blood. We manage our blood sugar levels with a hormone called insulin. To make sure that their blood sugar levels don't get too high, some diabetics have to inject themselves with insulin. The first known person with this condition was diagnosed in 1552 BC by Egyptian physician Hesy-Ra, after he noticed that his patient needed to go to the toilet a lot and was losing weight.

Way back in history, people also noticed that ants were attracted to the urine from people with these symptoms. Lucky individuals called "water tasters" would taste the pee of people with suspected diabetes. If it tasted sweet, they diagnosed diabetes! Nowadays, tests are a "wee" bit more scientific.

CHAPTER 9

GORGEOUS GUTS

Have you ever heard your tummy rumble and wondered what's going on in there? Well, the stomach and the brain work together when we're awake, when we're asleep, and when we're wondering what to eat next.

Why does your mouth water at the prospect of a yummy meal? Or why do you want to go to the toilet for a big poop? It's all here for you to explore, inside your **GORGEOUS GUTS.**

DISCOVERING DIGESTION

Your body gets all the energy and nutrients it needs from the food you eat. But where does that food go?

Grab a cookie. It's time to set off on the journey of a lifetime...through the digestive system!

Did you know it takes around eight seconds for the cookie you just chomped to travel from your mouth to your stomach?

1

MOUTH:
insert cookie
here!

2

TONGUE:
helps direct the
cookie toward
your throat

3

ESOPHAGUS:
down the slippery
slide to the
stomach!

4

STOMACH:
dissolves your
food in acid!

5

GALLBLADDER:
releases greeny-
yellow bile to help
break down fats

6

SMALL INTESTINE:
most digestion
happens here

7

LARGE INTESTINE:
watery waste is
absorbed here

8

RECTUM:
stores your poop
until you're
ready to go

9

ANUS:
the exit where
your poop
plops out!

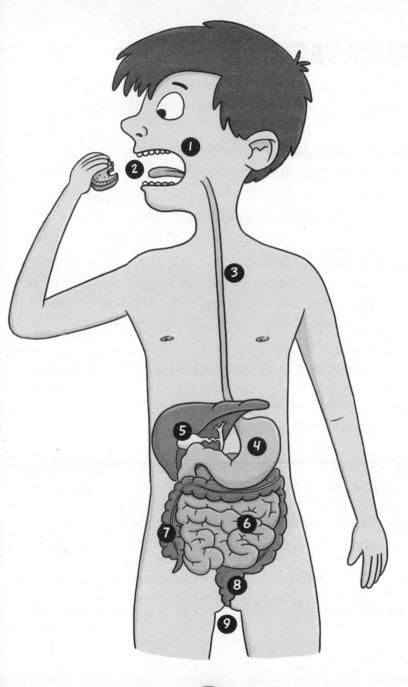

POOP FACTORY

Have you ever wondered how poop is made? Well, it all starts with...

SLIMY SALIVA

Also known as spit, this watery substance flows from glands in the mouth to moisten food, kill bacteria, and protect your throat from stomach acid.

BELLY BRILLIANCE

The stomach is a sack at the top of your abdomen that processes food. It's one of the most important parts of your body. Food gives us energy. But how?

- Food enters your esophagus with a big SWALLOW!

- It arrives in the stomach, and is broken down by chemicals called enzymes

- Your last meal can stay in the stomach for up to four hours

- Harmful microorganisms are destroyed in the stomach

- Then the food—or fuel—travels down the rest of your body to create...POWER!

Fascinating Facts!

☀ Your stomach can hold about four cups of chewed food.

☀ When you blush, your stomach lining does too!

TEAMWORK

The stomach relies on our brain. Our brains rely on the stomach. How does that work?

☀ Nerve signals are sent from the stomach to the brain...

☀ ...Or from the brain to the stomach! Ever had your mouth water when thinking about food?

☀ Once we've started eating, the brain tells us when we are full.

☀ To allow the brain to do its work, we need to eat... slowly.

DAZZLING DIGESTION!

From mouth to gut, and out through your butt ...

Stage 1
HOW THE COOKIE CRUMBLES

Once you chomp down on your cookie, proteins in your spit (called enzymes) begin to melt it down. Your tongue helps round up the crumbled cookie into one slimy blob, called a bolus, so it's easier to swallow. Once it's squishy enough, you can swallow, sending it tumbling down your super stomach chute—the esophagus.

Stage 2
STOMACH TIME, UNTIL IT'S CHYME

The muscles in your digestive system compress the bolus blob until it drops into your stomach. Once inside, gastric juices break it down further until it's a thick slimy paste, called chyme.

Fascinating Fact!

Your stomach has enough acid inside to dissolve metal! This acid can destroy bad bacteria in a flash and also liquifies your food. But why doesn't it burn a hole in your gut? MUCUS, of course. The inside layer is constantly replenished, stopping it from dissolving itself. It's a marvel of evolution!

Stage 3
NUTRIENT DOWNLOAD

The blob of chyme continues to move through your gorgeous guts, where your body absorbs everything it needs.

Welcome to your intestines. You have one that's small and one that's big! But how do they work?

☀ The small intestine sends nutrients into your blood stream using structures called villi.

☀ The large intestine turns waste into POOP!

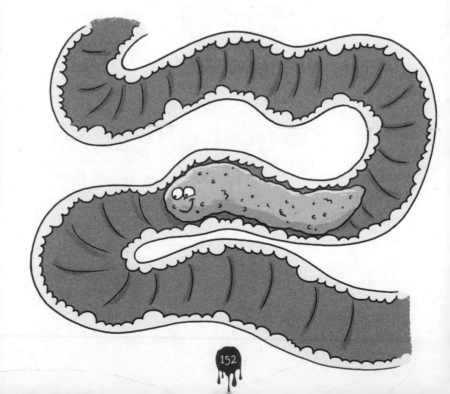

Stage 4
PERFECT POOP!

Finally, poop happens. When you eat, you'll need to excrete! We all do it. It's a fact of life. Excretion is the scientific word for getting rid of waste. Poopologists have fancy names for the brown stuff, like 'feces' or "stool." But it's all poop at the end of the day!

WHAT MAKES POOP?

Only a creepy clown could come up
with a recipe as GROSS as this!

WATER (around 75%)
SOLID MATTER (around 25%)

THE SOLID MATTER IS MADE UP OF:

INDIGESTIBLE FOOD MATTER—sometimes we
can't digest everything we eat, so it needs to
be expeled!

MARVELOUS MUCUS—some of the lining of our
gorgeous guts is taken on a one-way trip to
the toilet.

BACTERIA—there are a lot of them inside our
guts, so millions are dragged along for the ride!

Q. Why does your poop stink?

A. Bacteria break down our poop, making farty gases
like HYDROGEN SULFIDE. That's the same gas that
gives rotten eggs their stink!

SHAPING UP

Poop comes in many different shapes and sizes!
It can be...

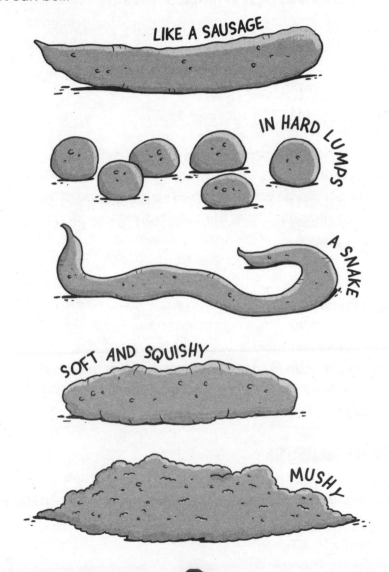

LIKE A SAUSAGE

IN HARD LUMPS

A SNAKE

SOFT AND SQUISHY

MUSHY

DISASTROUS DIARRHOEA

Diarrhoea is the medical word for "loose stool".
It usually doesn't last long—probably only a few days—
and is often caused by an infection of the intestines,
either from food poisoning or a virus. The body adds
more water to the poop recipe to help flush out the
invaders inside!

TAKEAWAY POOP

The main thing to understand is that everyone's poop
habits are unique to them. Your poop is YOUR poop!
Some people go to the toilet more often than others,
and that can be totally normal for them. As long as your
toilet habits are regular and you feel healthy, there's no
reason to be anything other than... **HAPPOOEY!**

SCENT OF ROSES

Let's face it, no poop is rose-scented. But it's
completely normal for your poop to smell bad. The
stink is caused by gases released by bacteria. But
sometimes the foods you eat can change your
poop's recipe!

BODY BLASTS!

It's not just poop that comes out of our awesome
bodies—we also release a variety of gross gases, thanks
to our digestion...

TOOT!

Um...excuse me!

BOOMING BURPS...

Belching, also known as burping, is your body's way of getting rid of excess air from your gorgeous guts. When we eat, we gulp down air at the same time, and we release it by letting out a massive BURP.

...AND FANTASTIC FARTS!

Flatulence is when gross gases escape from your bottom. Farts are also known as:

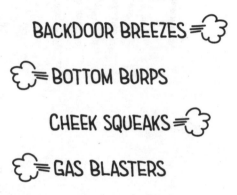

BACKDOOR BREEZES

BOTTOM BURPS

CHEEK SQUEAKS

GAS BLASTERS

Gases are formed when food is broken down inside your digestive system. They have to escape somewhere, otherwise you'd blow up like a balloon and float away into the clouds. OK, maybe not. BUT, your body needs to expel this gassy buildup somehow, so it lets it out the back door.

The gases that come out smell pretty bad, and can be worse depending on what you've eaten.

To make your farts smell **EXTRA BAD**, try eating more beans and onions.

After all ...

...BEANS, BEANS, GOOD FOR YOUR HEART.

THE MORE YOU EAT THEM, THE MORE YOU...

FART!

THE POOPBRUSH MYTH!

Have you ever heard that your toothbrush might be covered in poop? Less toothbrush, more poopbrush. According to the myth, every time you flush the toilet, the force sends poop particles floating around the bathroom—and some end up on your toothbrush.

Well, don't worry. Scientists did a research study testing toothbrushes for fecal bacteria—bacteria that could have only come from one place. And it turns out there are hardly any on your toothbrush, after all. Phew!

CHAPTER 10

BABY BOOM

From mammals and birds to reptiles, spiders, and even bacteria, all living things produce **OFFSPRING** by the process of reproduction.

Reproduction is **ESSENTIAL FOR LIFE**. Parents want their offspring to not only survive, but to thrive, so they can pass on their genes for generations to come.

The awesome organs and body parts that allow animals to make babies form the **REPRODUCTIVE SYSTEM.**

LIFE FINDS A WAY

There are two main types of reproduction:

1. ASEXUAL REPRODUCTION

...is when one animal creates offspring by itself. The offspring is called a clone. It is genetically identical to the parent (meaning it has the same genes).

This can involve:

Budding, when a growth called a bud breaks away from the animal to make a new animal. Corals, hydras, and sea anemones do this.

Fragmentation, when a body breaks into different pieces (fragments). Some worms can split in half to make two separate animals. Starfish can form from a single arm that breaks away from the parent.

2. SEXUAL REPRODUCTION

...is when two sex cells fuse (join together) to make a baby. One cell is from a female, and the other is from a male. This process is called fertilization.

* In most animals, including mammals, the sex cells fuse INSIDE the female's body. After the sex cells fuse, they grow and develop into a baby.

* The offspring of some animals, such as birds or reptiles, develop in eggs OUTSIDE the female's body. The female bird or reptile lays the fertilized eggs, and watches over them until they hatch.

Humans make babies through sexual reproduction, just like other mammals. A woman's body provides everything the baby needs to grow and develop.

Males and females have different reproductive organs and genitals—these are a person's external organ of reproduction, such as the vulva in a woman, or the penis in a man.

FANTASTIC FEMALES

A baby girl is born with all the eggs she'll ever have—more than 500,000 eggs in each ovary, over a million in total!

EGG-cellent Information!

- The scientific name for an egg is an ovum.

- Egg cells are the largest cells in the human body. They have a diameter of around 0.1mm. This means they're twenty times bigger than sperm cells!

- Egg cells start off as immature, meaning they still need to develop. Only mature egg cells are released during the process of ovulation.

- If an egg is not fertilised, it has a short lifespan - no longer than 2 weeks.

- Freezing eggs doesn't damage them. This means women can have their eggs extracted (taken out) and frozen. These eggs can then be used to get pregnant many years later!

FEMALE REPRODUCTIVE SYSTEM

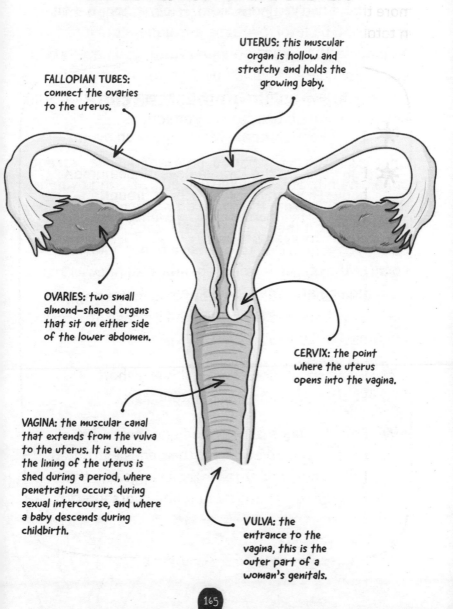

UTERUS: this muscular organ is hollow and stretchy and holds the growing baby.

FALLOPIAN TUBES: connect the ovaries to the uterus.

OVARIES: two small almond-shaped organs that sit on either side of the lower abdomen.

CERVIX: the point where the uterus opens into the vagina.

VAGINA: the muscular canal that extends from the vulva to the uterus. It is where the lining of the uterus is shed during a period, where penetration occurs during sexual intercourse, and where a baby descends during childbirth.

VULVA: the entrance to the vagina, this is the outer part of a woman's genitals.

ONCE A MONTH

A young woman usually starts having periods when she's about twelve years old. This can happen a bit earlier or a bit later, because everyone is unique. As a guide, this usually happens after you have grown underarm hair and pubic hair. But whenever you get there, you have entered a whole other fascinating stage of being a human being. Congratulations!

Once a girl starts her period, an ovary releases an egg, once a month. This is called ovulation. During ovulation, the egg moves from the ovary down the fallopian tube to the uterus. If the egg is not fertilized, it dies. This is perfectly normal. Due to a release of hormones, the lining of the uterus is released, taking the egg with it. Both the egg and some blood pass out of the uterus and through the vagina in a process known as "having your period." The cycle starts all over again the following month.

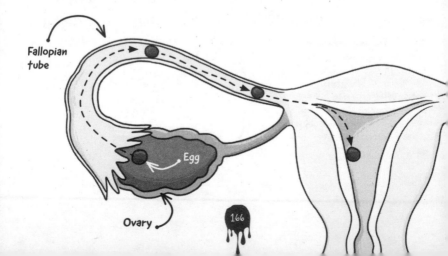

Fallopian tube

Egg

Ovary

PERIOD PREPARATION

Starting your periods can be startling, but most young women go through this.

Here are some of the details to understand about your changing body...

- You'll lose about 3-5 tablespoons of blood with every period.

- You might have some tummy pain, which can be a surprise.

- Be prepared! Of course, this isn't easy, when your first period might come out of nowhere. Why not talk to friends about what help they have found?

- Chat to teachers or school nurses. They'll understand.

- And if you know someone close to you who is going through this stage, be supportive. We can all help each other, always.

TESTING THE TESTES

In males, the main reproductive organs are the testes. The two oval-shaped testicles sit behind the penis, in a pouch called the scrotum. This is a very useful set of equipment, because testes make the male sex cells, called sperm.

Sperm Specifics

- Sperm are shaped like tadpoles, with long tails.

- More than 50 MILLION sperm swim to engage with a single egg.

- But only ONE crosses the finish line!

- Sperm swim at speeds of $\frac{1}{8}$ inch per minute—fast considering how tiny they are, at just 0.065mm in length!

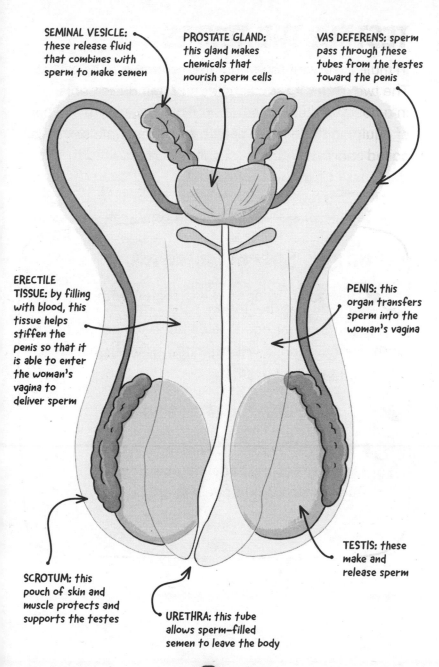

SEMINAL VESICLE: these release fluid that combines with sperm to make semen

PROSTATE GLAND: this gland makes chemicals that nourish sperm cells

VAS DEFERENS: sperm pass through these tubes from the testes toward the penis

ERECTILE TISSUE: by filling with blood, this tissue helps stiffen the penis so that it is able to enter the woman's vagina to deliver sperm

PENIS: this organ transfers sperm into the woman's vagina

TESTIS: these make and release sperm

SCROTUM: this pouch of skin and muscle protects and supports the testes

URETHRA: this tube allows sperm-filled semen to leave the body

MAKING A BABY

During sexual intercourse, when a man and a woman come together, a small amount of semen passes through the penis into the woman's vagina. This semen, containing nearly **100 million sperm**, moves up through the uterus and into the fallopian tubes toward the woman's egg. If the sperm meet an egg, they try to fuse with it. Only one sperm can enter, or fertilize, the egg. The remaining sperm—**all 99,999,999 of them**—die!

GESTATION

After the egg is fertilized, pregnancy—also called gestation—begins. Gestation is the time period that a mother carries her baby inside her body before giving birth. For humans, this is typically nine whole months.

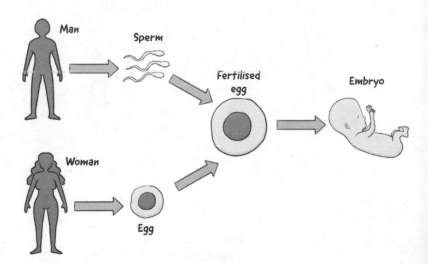

BOYS' CHANGES

As a young man goes through puberty, he experiences various changes. These can include having erections. This is when the penis hardens due to increased blood flow in its spongy tissues, making it become larger and stand up from the body.

Another change a boy can experience is sometimes called a "wet dream." This is when he ejaculates during sleep. Ejaculation is when semen (a milky fluid containing sperm) comes out of the head of an erect penis. After ejaculation, the penis will go soft again. This is all a completely normal part of growing up! As a boy's hormones settle down, he'll have fewer unexpected erections and wet dreams.

THE GROWING FETUS

Once fertilized, the human egg divides. One cell becomes two. Two become four, and so on.

The new clump of cells burrow into the wall of the uterus and develop into a baby.

✳ **At first, the developing cells are called an embryo.**

✳ **After about eight weeks, the cells become a fetus.**

The baby grows inside a pouch called the amniotic sac, which is filled with a clear liquid called amniotic fluid. This fluid protects the baby as it grows.

The baby is connected to their mother by a bundle of blood vessels called the umbilical cord. The cord connects the baby's belly to an awesome organ called the placenta. The placenta is super important: it transfers food and oxygen from mother to baby, while also allowing the baby's waste to be transported away.

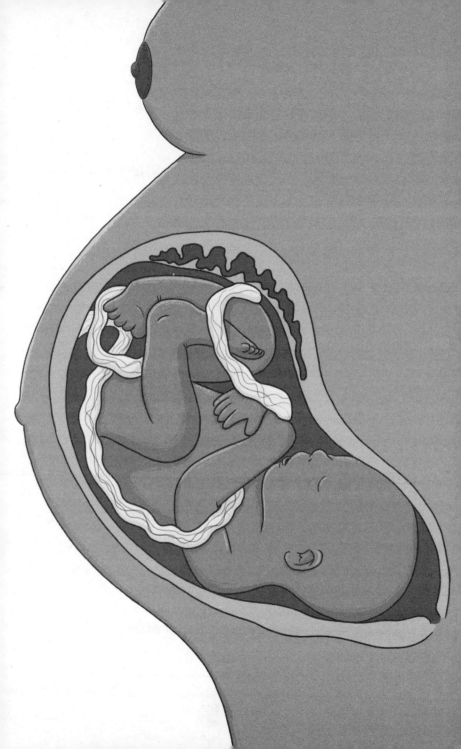

WELCOME TO THE WORLD

After around nine months, a baby is ready to come into the world!

When a woman begins labor—or giving birth—the cervix (the bottom end of the uterus) opens and expands to create a wide opening into the vagina. This happens in waves called contractions.

As time goes on, the contractions speed up. The muscles of the uterus tighten to push the baby toward the opening. The baby moves slowly through the vagina and out of the mother's body. The umbilical cord is cut, and the baby has arrived!

Fascinating baby facts!

* Human babies are born without kneecaps.

* A baby blue whale can put on 22 lb per hour— the same weight as a car tire.

* Newborn piglets recognize their mother's voice within two weeks of being born.

* Seahorse dads give birth, not moms!

Animal Gestation

The time it takes to make a baby varies
throughout the animal world!

(shortest in the world!)

Virginian opossum	12 days
Centipede	4 weeks
Squirrel	6 weeks
Tarantula	6 weeks
Snake	6 weeks
Chimpanzee	8 months
Gorilla	8.5 months
Human	9 months
Manatee	13 months
Camel	13–15 months
Giraffe	15 months
Velvet worm	15 months
Dolphin	17 months
Sperm whale	19 months
Indian elephant	22 months

The creation of new life is wonderful. But the way some organisms reproduce is not quite so nice...

GROSS GROWTH!

A barnacle called *rhizocephalans*—rhizo for short—has a gross way of bringing its babies into the world. Each rhizo floats around the ocean until it comes across a poor female crab, and latches onto her shell. It grows little syringe-like lumps and drills them into the crab's shell. It scrambles inside the crab's nose and sets up home!

The rhizo grows an extensive root system throughout the crab's body, until these strange roots reach the cavity where the crab holds her eggs. The rhizo continues to grow, taking control of many of the crab's functions. As the rhizo sucks the crab of energy, she slowly becomes sterile, meaning her eggs are no longer functional. Poor crab mama!

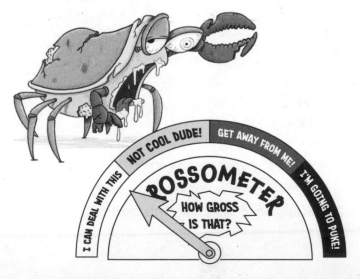

I CAN DEAL WITH THIS — NOT COOL DUDE! — GET AWAY FROM ME! — I'M GOING TO PUKE!

GROSSOMETER

HOW GROSS IS THAT?

CHAPTER 11

MARVELOUS MINDS, SWEET DREAMS

Something special separates humans from the rest of the animal kingdom. It's our **CREATIVE, INTELLIGENT MIND!**

It allows us to access speech, consciousness, tool use, and culture. And that's just the start! The famous British playwright Shakespeare explained it best:

"WHAT A PIECE OF WORK IS A MAN! HOW NOBLE IN REASON! HOW INFINITE IN FACULTY!"
Hamlet, Act 2, scene 2

So, let's find out exactly what Shakespeare was talking about...

TWO FOR ONE

Your **BRAIN** and your **MIND** both inhabit the same part of your body...but they are different. **HOW?**

A **BRAIN** is built of physical matter—it's the blob of meat inside your skull.

Your **MIND** is made up of:

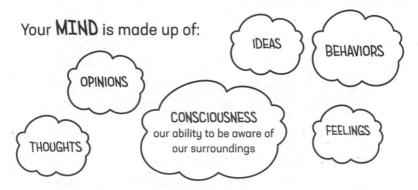

IDEAS

BEHAVIORS

OPINIONS

CONSCIOUSNESS
our ability to be aware of
our surroundings

FEELINGS

THOUGHTS

These acts of the mind all stem from your brilliant brain, but they don't physically exist. Just think, there's a part of you that's invisible—what is going on inside your head!

This is why we are different as human beings. Our intelligence represents our ability to learn from experience, adapt to new situations, understand different concepts, and use knowledge to make changes. Developing intelligence was vital for Lucy millions of years ago when she first started using tools to hunt. Lucy's intelligence allowed her to adapt, and this led to...human evolution!

AMAZING ADAPTORS

The ability to adapt means that a person can learn new skills and behaviors in response to a change in circumstances.

Adapting involves lots of different thoughts, sometimes at the same time. Below are just a few of them. Can you match the right label with the correct description?

PERCEPTION

LEARNING

MEMORY

REASONING

PROBLEM SOLVING

A. the ability to acquire new knowledge, understanding, behaviors, or skills

B. the ability to think about something in a logical way

C. the ability of the brain to store and retrieve information

D. the ability to see, hear, or become aware of something through our sensational senses

E. finding solutions to problems or difficulties

Answers: Perception: D, Learning: A, Memory: C, Reasoning: B, Problem Solving: E

MINDS AND BODIES

Your magical mind and amazing body are best friends. They're linked, meaning how you think or feel can affect how your body performs. This is called the mind-body connection.

Here are just some of the ways this can work:

✸ **Butterflies in your tummy when you feel nervous.**

✸ **A shudder when you imagine something gross.**

✸ **Blushing when you feel embarrassed.**

✸ **Yawning at the end of a long day.**
(Fun fact—no one knows why we yawn!)

Can you think of any other ways your mind connects with your body?

Mind-Body In Reverse!

You can work things back-to-front, too, and use your body to affect your mind. For example, if you take deep breaths, you can calm a busy mind. Over time, your mind will learn that this is what a deep breath means, and immediately calm down. If that doesn't work, you can find a supporter to talk to— a friend, teacher, or family member. Remember, all emotions are valid.

SLEEP SCIENCE

Sleep is the single most effective thing we can do to reset our brain and body health each day. It's essential for healthy bodies and minds. It impacts our thoughts, feelings, and emotions so it's important to get a good night's sleep!

Did you know that within a minute of falling asleep, your body starts to change?

☀ **Your temperature drops**

☀ **Your brain activity fizzles down**

☀ **Your heart rate and breathing rate slow too!**

Sleep is not as simple as closing your eyes and nodding off. There are four different stages of sleep, called cycles. These cycles are fundamental to how sleep works.

SLEEP CYCLES

1. Dozing off:
Getting sleepy in 3...2...1...and...

z z Z Z Z Z

2. Slow down:
We've dozed off, but we still can be easily woken up here.

3. Non-REM sleep:
REM stands for Rapid Eye Movement but we're not there yet. In non-REM sleep, we're not yet in a deep sleep. Here, your body relaxes more, and your brain waves start to change, slowing down.

4. REM sleep:
Brain activity shoots up again, and our whole body goes into a state of temporary paralysis, meaning we can't move. This is to protect us from acting out our dreams! The only parts of the body not paralyzed are the eyes (rapid eye movement!) and our breathing muscles.

READY FOR REM SLEEP!

- ☀ REM sleep is important for our memory and learning.

- ☀ Most people dream for about two hours each night.

- ☀ You probably don't remember most of your dreams.

- ☀ Dreams can happen during any stage of sleep, but they happen more during REM sleep.

- ☀ Dreams during REM sleep are usually vivid, bizarre, and even fantastical! Think zombie fights, creepy clown chases, alien invasions, or space battles! What did you dream last night? Write it down and share it with your friends!

SWEET DREAMS

Dreams are the most fascinating aspects of sleep, involving images, thoughts, and feelings. There isn't a clear explanation for their meaning or purpose.

* Most dreams consist of some form of visual images, but they can involve all of the senses.

* Some people dream in color, while others dream in black and white.

* Blind people tend to have dreams involving their other senses, such as sound, taste, and smell.

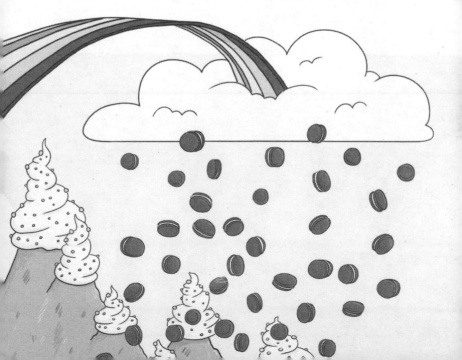

DREAM TEAM

Scientists are still researching what the purpose of dreams are, but they could be important for:

* Building memories

* Processing our emotions

* Organizing our thoughts

NASTY NIGHTMARES

Any dream associated with negative feelings, such as anxiety or fear, is a nightmare. Some nightmares are easy to deal with. Like when that creepy clown chased you down the road. It wasn't real, and you were safe in your bed!

But some nightmares could represent fears and worries in your daily life—like an upcoming test, for example. If this is the case, remember it's good to share your dreams and worries with someone, and lighten the load!

SMART AS A PIG?

Humans are not the only intelligent beings on Planet Earth. **Animal cognition** is an amazing branch of biology that studies how animals:

- Think

- Communicate

- Understand concepts

- Show empathy (understand others' feelings)

- Solve problems

Animals that have shown remarkable intelligence include:

- Rats
- Pigeons
- Crows
- Pigs
- Octopuses

- African grey parrots
- Elephants
- Chimpanzees
- Bottlenose dolphins
- Orangutans

Fascinating Facts!

☀ Pigs and rats are both as intelligent as dogs!

☀ The octopus is the only invertebrate animal to make our smart list. (Invertebrate means that it has no backbone.)

☀ An elephant has the largest brain of any land animal.

☀ Dolphins are one of the few animals that can recognize themselves in a mirror!

☀ A dog can be as intelligent as a two-year-old human!

189

ANIMAL CELEBRITIES

ALEX THE GREY PARROT

was born in 1976 and was the subject of many studies. He was so smart that he could recognise colors, shapes, and objects such as keys. Alex could even recognize different numbers!

AKEAKAMAI THE DOLPHIN

could recognize different gestures made by her human handler's arms and hands. She learned some words and eventually strings of words—which could be described as sentences, such as "take the ball to the hoop!"

Ocean's Eight

Octopuses are one of the smartest animals in the ocean, and they have good memories. They can solve problems, navigate through mazes, and they even play games!

Although the octopuses' nervous system has a central brain, a large proportion of their nerves form a network throughout their eight arms, serving as eight extra "mini brains." No wonder they're so smart!

Octopuses are so intelligent, many countries now recognize them as sentient beings—meaning they can perceive and feel things!

MIND CONTROL: FUNGUS STYLE!

Deep inside the Brazilian rainforest, you may come across an acrobatic ant, hanging onto a leaf using only its jaws. The ant has inhaled the spores of the *Ophiocordyceps unilateralis* fungus and become a zombie ant, controlled by the fungus!

An infected zombie ant feels compelled—or controlled—to leave its home and climb any nearby plant. Acting under the mind control of the fungus, the ant locks its jaws onto a leaf. This action signals to the fungus that it's time to make its last killer move. It sends a stalk bursting through the ant's outer layers!

The stalk then explodes, sprinkling fungal spores down to the forest floor. The spores rain down onto the rest of its ant family, zombifying the rest of them one by one...

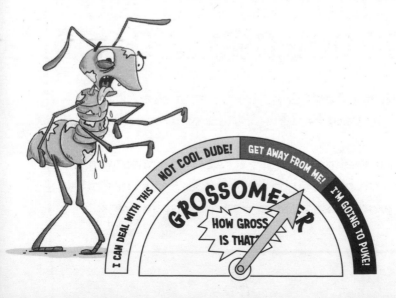

I CAN DEAL WITH THIS

NOT COOL DUDE!

GET AWAY FROM ME!

I'M GOING TO PUKE!

GROSSOMETER

HOW GROSS IS THAT?

CHAPTER 12

BODY BEAUTIFUL

You're a **MARVEL OF EVOLUTION,** a completely **UNIQUE HUMAN BEING!**

You're made up of

7,000,000,000,000, 000,000,000,000,000

(that's 7 octillion) atoms, and every atom in your body is billions of years old.

That makes you **SPECIAL**. But sometimes, it can be easy to forget this. Let's remind ourselves how extraordinary you are!

WHAT IS BODY IMAGE?

Body image is the way we see ourselves. You might:

* compare how you look with other people

* hide your body because you don't like it

* struggle to find clothes to fit you

* be worried about birthmarks, scars, or acne

* feel as though your body does not match your gender

WHAT IS BODY POSITIVITY?

Body positivity is about accepting all bodies, just the way they are. All people deserve to feel positive about the way they look. They're unique, and special, after all. Here are some small things YOU can do every day to be more BODY POSITIVE:

* Help your friends like their appearance. "Hey, you look awesome!"

* Find a compliment for someone that isn't about their body. What about their brain, or their kindness?

* Avoid negative words to talk about any body—yours or a friend's.

194

- In fact, stop and think about whether or not you really **NEED** to talk about someone else's body. It's their body, after all!

- Challenge people who are unkind with their words.

- Remember that the perfect bodies we see on our screens aren't always the real picture—even social media stars use apps to make them look "better."

- Remind yourself and everyone that...

THERE IS NO PERFECT BODY!

MIND YOUR MIND

The way we see our body and how we think and feel about ourselves is called **self-esteem**. It isn't just about our appearance, but also how confident we feel. When we have good self-esteem, we:

- believe we're worthy and deserving of good things in life

- recognize and value the skills and abilities we have

- are not worried about what others think of us

- are not worried about making mistakes

- feel comfortable sharing our opinions and ideas

- believe what we have to say matters

- treat ourselves kindly

But sometimes, we might find it hard to believe in ourselves or feel good enough. That's OK. It's normal to struggle with our self-esteem, and this can change at different times in our lives.

Self-esteem

The first person to come up with the concept of self-esteem was an American scientist named William James. He did this way back in 1890, in a book that took him twelve years to write! This makes self-esteem one of the oldest concepts in psychology, the science of the mind.

SLAP!

WHO AM I?

Knowing who you are is not always easy. Some people know who they are at a young age. Others may take years or even decades! That's because everyone is different.

Here are some questions to ask yourself:

1. Do you know what you find easy to do, and what you find difficult?

2. Are you neat, tidy, and well organized, or are you messy and lose things easily?

3. Do you find yourself worrying a lot, or not at all? If you can answer these questions, then you already have very good self-awareness. Don't worry if you don't though, you will develop more self-awareness as you get older.

UNDERSTANDING DIFFERENCES

We're all different, and that's part of being human.
Here are some of our differences:

- Age

- Sex assigned at birth

- Eye color

- Skin color

- Hair type

- Ethnicity (culture, language, and community)

- Gender identity

- Attraction to others (sexual orientation)

- Neurodivergence (different types of brilliant brain)

- Physical abilities or disabilities

- How we learn or process thoughts

- Physical or mental health

- Religious beliefs

People's differences may mean they face additional
challenges in life.

WE'RE ALL UNIQUE

Sara Rankin is a professor of leukocyte and stem cell biology. Throughout her school life, she found ways to make sure she achieved the grades she hoped for. She would use visual clues and patterns to help her memorize things. It was only later in life that she realized she'd been living with learning differences. Sara has now embraced her neurodiversity and believes that the determination and strength it has given her unlocked the key to her success.

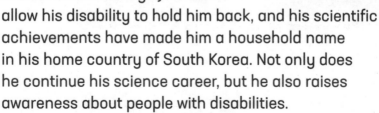

Sang-Mook Lee is a professor of oceanography. He spent years researching the oceans. One day, his life was changed forever when an accident left him quadriplegic. (This means that he was paralyzed in both arms and legs.) He didn't allow his disability to hold him back, and his scientific achievements have made him a household name in his home country of South Korea. Not only does he continue his science career, but he also raises awareness about people with disabilities.

Rose Ayling-Ellis is a British actress and the first deaf person to win Strictly Come Dancing, along with her dance partner, Giovanni Pernice. One of their winning dances featured a period of silence during which they kept dancing. This detail was included as a tribute to the deaf community—and was awarded the UK's "TV moment of the year" in 2021.

A BETTER WORLD

Together, we want to work toward a world where everyone is celebrated for their differences, and all people, whatever their background, have the same opportunities. We're a long way from achieving this, which means that all of us have a responsibility to work together towards this goal.

WONDERFUL WELLBEING

Imagine your body is a car. Well, it is the vehicle that drives your marvelous mind around!

☀ You need to use the car regularly to make sure it continues working properly

☀ You need to give it the right fuel

So how do we do this?

1. MOVE MORE—IF YOU CAN

☀ Try to get some physical activity every day. Walking, dancing, skipping...they all count!

☀ Be active at home: help with the gardening or even SHOCK, HORROR! changing your bed sheets.

☀ Go on a family walk after your dinner.

☀ Hike, cycle, or swim when you go on vacation.

☀ Reduce TV, computer, and videogame time.

2. EAT WELL

Eating a healthy, balanced diet is essential for maintaining good health. Not only that, but it makes you feel great too!

FRUIT AND VEGETABLES: eat at least five portions every day to load up on vitamins and minerals.

CARBOHYDRATES: potatoes, breads, grains, rice, or pasta give you energy.

PROTEIN: this helps you grow! You can find it in beans, fish, eggs, or meat.

FIBER: rye crackers, unsalted nuts, and seeds all keep your digestive system moving.

DAIRY: milk and cheese, or fortified alternatives such as oat, coconut, or soya milks, help build your bones.

OILS: choose unsaturated oils and spreads, and eat them in small amounts for essential fats and vitamins.

Oh, and to help that all go down, make sure you drink at least six to eight glasses of water a day!

Right For You?

Remember: some people may have allergies or diet restrictions, so always check to make sure what you eat is right for you. If you're not sure, speak to a parent and they can take you to a dietitian or doctor for a chat.

MARVELOUS MICROBIOME!

There's something else that makes you, you. It's microbiomes—which are communities of microorganisms living **ON YOU** and **INSIDE YOU**!

The microbiome includes both helpful and potentially harmful microbes. Most are symbiotic (helpful to the body) while some are pathogenic (meaning they can cause disease). In a healthy body, these two types generally coexist without any problems. But sometimes, the balance is lost, and more pathogenic bacteria can grow, leading to health issues. This can be an issue for people with weakened immune systems.

Examples of microbial communities include:

- **Bacteria and fungi on the surface of your super skin**

- **Bacteria inside your gorgeous guts**

The gut microbiome includes all the microbes inside your intestines! These belly bacteria help to:

- **Digest food**

- **Regulate the immune system**

- **Maintain a good nervous system and brain health**

Fascinating facts!

✹ Most of the skin microbiome lives on your epidermis—the outer layers of skin.

✹ Forget nits, think microbiome! They live inside your hair follicles.

✹ There are about 100 TRILLION bacteria in the gut.

✹ There are more bacterial cells in your body than human cells!

SIX STEPS TO SUCCEED...

1.

Your body is yours and yours alone—
own it. Even your boogers.

2.

We're all different. We're all beautiful. But it's
your **THOUGHTS** and **ACTIONS** that make
you who you are. Not the way you look.

3.

Be confident, creative, and live in the present
moment. The past is history, and the future
is unwritten. **LIVE NOW**.

...IN YOUR SKIN

4.

Be Kind. Kindness always wins.

5.

Stop comparing yourself to others. Only then, will you realize how UNIQUE and SPECIAL you truly are.

6.

And most importantly, remember about 56 percent of your body's cells are bacteria, and only 44 percent are human. That makes you a little bit GROSS.

But it's also why you're PERFECT, just the way you are.

207

Wait—did we say there are more bacterial cells than human cells in you...?

This is way too much information...even for the
GROSSOMETER! We've broken it!